Eurotunnel Drinkbuyer's Guide

by Martin Daltrop

To David
with love
1996
Annette

B❦XTREE

First published in Great Britain in 1995 by
Boxtree Limited, Broadwall House, 21 Broadwall, London SE1 9PL

Text © Martin Daltrop
Map by Raymond Turvey
Jacket illustration by Karen Elliott

1 3 5 7 9 10 8 6 4 2

ISBN 0 7522 1696 1

Designed by Robert Updegraff
Typeset by SX Composing Ltd, Rayleigh, Essex
Printed and bound in Great Britain by
Cox & Wyman, Reading, Berks.

A CIP catalogue entry for this book
is available from the British Library

CONTENTS

Part 2 – The Shops

Introduction

Drink is significantly more expensive in Britain than on the continental side of the Channel, but since 1993 there has been no limit to the amount that you may bring back. If ever you wondered why they went to all that trouble to build the Channel Tunnel, the answer should be obvious: large amounts of cheap drink can now be brought back to Britain in double quick time.

This book tells you what to buy and where to buy it. It lists the best places to shop within one hour's drive of the Channel Tunnel along with information about where to stay and what to see. The area covered takes in not only shops near to Calais - where you might go with the sole purpose of loading up with drink - but also places further afield, where you can combine drink-buying with a wonderful week-end of eating, sight-seeing and relaxing.

There are certainly big savings to be made, but crossing the Channel also offers a far greater choice of certain things. Many French wines, particularly those from outside the main growing regions, are hard or impossible to find in Britain. There is also a wide variety of fortified wines, spirits and Belgian beers that we never see in British shops. Then there is the experience of buying itself; you can buy wine from châteaux and ancient cellars, or beer from monasteries and specialist shops, which is a lot more enjoyable and memorable than visiting the High Street offie.

The choice of what to buy is as difficult as where to buy it, so in addition to information about the shops the book describes the different wines, beers and spirits that you will come across and offers advice on what to buy.

THE LAW

January 1993 saw the introduction of the Single European Act which opened up internal borders and began the process of harmonization in rates of duty on alcoholic drinks across the European Community. By 1999 no difference in rates of VAT and duty between member states should exist, and, although that is extremely unlikely to happen on time, import controls between member states have been removed.

The one caveat to this, however, is that alcohol bought in other countries cannot be resold in the UK. Although customs controls as such have been terminated, we may still have to prove that what we have bought is for our personal use. In practice, this could be quite tricky. How can you tell from the look of a bottle who is going to consume it? What you can infer, however, is that few of us, even if we had loads of friends, would be able to consume a million bottles of beer before they reach their drink-by date, and the chances are that some could find their way into car boot sales up and down the country. So, quantity is used as an indication of whether goods are intended for personal use or not, and to try to make life easier, guidelines called MILs (Minimum Indicative Limits) have been drawn up to suggest what is a reasonable quantity for an individual to bring back. These currently stand at:

* 90 litres still wine of which 60 may be sparkling
* plus 110 litres of beer
* plus 20 litres of fortified wine
* plus 10 litres of spirits.

It must be stressed, however, that these are only guidelines, limits below which you can bring drink back into Britain with no questions asked. More alcohol than recommended in the guidelines may be brought back but you need a reason and possibly some proof to offer as explanation. For example, a party or a wedding would be an acceptable reason, and a sample invitation or clear details about it should be satisfactory proof. Although it is all fairly vague at the moment, it is definitely worth thinking about how you might explain to a customs officer why you have brought back more than set down in the guidelines.

Remember that this is for drink for which duty has been paid. It is different for duty free drinks, which may only be bought in special shops between borders. Duty free shops still exist between continental Europe and Britain. If you want a litre of spirits and 2 litres of fortified wine - which is the allowance for these products - then you will make savings buying them in a duty free shop.

THE SAVINGS

In France you pay about £1.10 less in tax per bottle of wine compared with the UK, £1.80 less on a bottle of sparkling wine, £2.80 less on a bottle of spirits, 45p less on a bottle of fortified wine and about 35p less on a pint of beer. In Belgium the savings are a little less than in France on beer, and a little greater on fortified wine and spirits. They are, however, significantly less on wine. On a full allowance of wine, beer and spirits, you would save around £200 on the duty alone. By carefully choosing what you buy, the savings can be a lot greater.

HOW MUCH TO BRING BACK?

Although the more drink you bring back the more money you save, you are likely to be limited by the space in your vehicle. It is well worth doing the calculations before you leave, to check you have enough space to buy a sufficient quantity of the drink you require to make the trip worthwhile. If you intend to buy plonk and you are travelling in a Mini, you may have to think again. Even if your car is fairly large, it might be worth hiring a van, or joining up with a friend and hiring one between two. It is not just space which may be at a premium, weight can be a problem too. Drink is quite heavy, with a case of wine weighing around 16kg and with sparkling wine being much heavier. Check the maximum pay-load of your vehicle and work out if it will cope with the weight. It would be very depressing to buy a large quantity of wine at a great saving and then realize that you couldn't get it home.

HOW TO USE THIS BOOK

This book is divided into two sections. Part 1 describes the different drinks available and gives advice on what is good value. Chapter 1 gives general advice on buying wine, and Chapters 2-12 describe wines from various regions of the world that you will see in the shops. Chapter 13 looks at beer and cider, while Chapter 14 deals with different types of fortified wines and spirits. Part 2 covers the shops themselves. The area within one hour's drive of Calais is divided into three parts; Chapter 15 deals with the area south of the Tunnel, Chapter 16 describes the area south-east of the Tunnel and Chapter 17 looks at the area north of the Tunnel. The shops are arranged in order along the route being followed. Within each town, they are ordered alphabetically. Finally, in the appendices there are recommendations for the best wines, beers and spirits to look out for and the best shops in which to buy them, as well as a glossary and information about the Channel Tunnel.

Route 1	Time from mouth of French side of tunnel in minutes
Calais	10
Frethun	5
Ardres	15
Recques sur Mer	20
St Omer	30
Aire sur la Lys	35
Lillers	40
Bethune	45
Bruay en Artois	45

Route 2	
Wissant	15
Wimille	20
Wimereux	20
Boulogne	25
Samer	40

Le Touquet	45
Etaples	45
St Pol sur Ternoise	60
Loison sur Crequoise	70
Hesdin	70
Arras	60
Berck Plage	55
Montreuil	50
Beaurainville	60

Route 3

Dunkerque	30
Bergues	40
Westvleteren	60
Poperinge	60
Lille	75
Veurne	45
Westende	55
Nieuwpoort	55
Oostende	60
Diksmuide	60
Bruges	75
Middelkerke	60

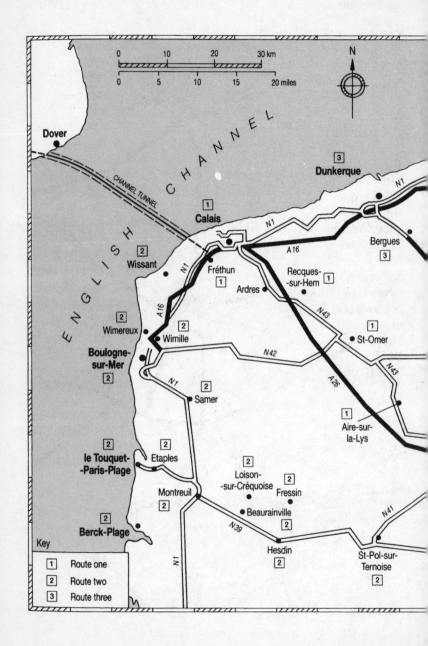

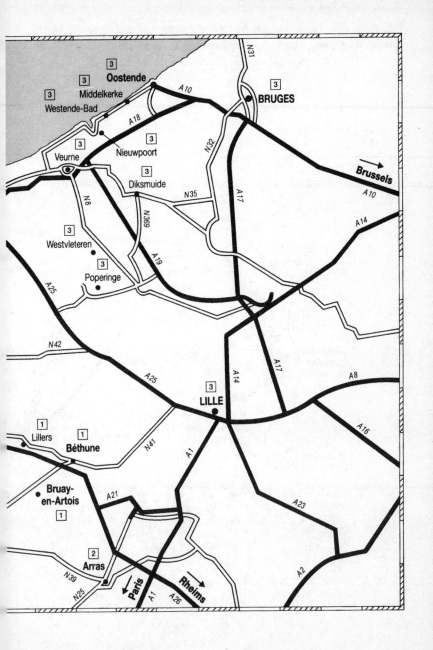

EXCHANGE RATES

Prices in this book are given in the currency as displayed in the shop being described. At the time of writing the exchange rate was approximately £1 to 8 F (French francs) to 50 BF (Belgian francs).

PART 1
THE DRINKS

CHAPTER 1

Buying Wine

Choosing wine can be an intimidating experience; we are supposed to be knowledgeable and serious, and know what we want. In wine shops, it can seem like the sales people are not there to put us at ease and to help, but to test our wine knowledge and good taste. Confronted with this, we play safe, and ask for a name that we've heard of or tried before: a Chablis, a Chardonnay, a Beaujolais, anything so as not to appear foolish. In the supermarket there is no feeling of pressure but a mass of names appearing randomly before us. What is the relationship between all the different names on the bottles: Chateau, Chablis, Chardonnay? It feels like it's terribly important and not knowing is disconcerting.

Yet, drinking wine is enjoyable, and buying it should be too. Maybe we shouldn't take it so seriously. This doesn't mean that we need not consider, choose carefully and be conscious of what we buy. We just need to know what to look out for and how to make basic decisions, such as:

* How much do we want to spend?
* What style of wine would we like?
* What occasion is the wine intended for?
* Is the wine to drink now, or to keep?

HOW MUCH?

People sometimes get quite offended when they are asked in a shop how much they want to spend, and they often reply quite testily; 'It doesn't matter, I want something really good, the price isn't important.' In reality though, the price is important. That is not to say you cannot be overcharged for something horrible, or that you can't find great bargains, but price is clearly an indicator of quality. Wines in France range from a few francs a bottle to several hundred, or even thousands. So why the difference? A lot of it is down to the quality; the quality of the fruit, the care and attention that goes into the making, the skills and experience of the maker, the use of oak, the cellaring and so on. These are very real differences. However, there is also the effect of supply and demand, fashion, marketing and promotion. These can artificially raise prices. Whether a top Bordeaux is worth 20 times a very drinkable red plonk is impossible to say.

In the chapters listing wines from various regions, the wines are divided up into three price categories: **Low**, £2.50 (20 F or 125 BF) and under; **Mid**, from £2.50 to £7.50 (60 F or 375 BF); and **High**, from 60 F upwards. At the lower end of the market I think you need to pay a little more for drinkable white wine than for red. Generally, white wine of less than 12 F and red wine of less than 8 F are not to be recommended. There are a number of exceptions however.

Low-Priced Wine

There is plenty of good drinking wine available in the **Low** category, and this is the wine where the biggest savings can be made relative to the UK. This is because as duty is a flat rate and not a percentage, it represents a much higher proportion of the cost of a cheap item than an expensive one. So if duty represents a difference of £1.10 per bottle, you would save 40% on the cost of a bottle of wine normally costing £2.75 in Britain. Spend £100 on this type of wine and you have saved £40. On a bottle of wine which costs £11, however, the saving on duty would be only 10%.

More Expensive Wine

For really good wine you have to move into the **Mid** category, and here again massive savings can be made. Wine in the **High** category may not be cheaper than in Britain, because the duty now becomes quite a small proportion of the cost of the bottle. However, a great deal of champagne and other sparkling wine in the High price bracket will almost certainly be significantly cheaper.

Whatever the price category of the wine you are buying, it is important to remember that items which the locals buy in bulk are going to be good value compared to those they don't. French people drink mainly French wine so the market for non-French wine is not nearly as competitive as in the UK. On non-French wine, although the savings can be significant, they will only represent the differences in duty between France and Britain. On certain French wines the prices will also reflect the effect of a very competitive local market for that product.

Wine en Vrac

It is possible to find very good value cheap wine **en Vrac**. This means it is sold straight from something that looks like a petrol pump, in large containers. Wine sold like this can be amazingly cheap, often starting at 6 F a litre. Buying wine like this might be ideal for a party or some event where it is consumed shortly after getting back. This is because the containers are usually cheap and not airtight and won't keep the wine more than a few days unless it is bottled. It is possible to bottle the wine yourself once back home, but I have heard varying reports on how easy it is; some people say it is straightforward but others insist it is a complicated process requiring sterilization of the bottles. If you don't mind experimenting, it might be good fun to try.

A much easier solution, however, seems to be to buy good-quality reusable vacuum boxes which keep the wine for up to three months. These are sold in many of the shops that sell wine en Vrac (see Part 2: The Shops).

Advantages of buying the wine en Vrac apart from the low price is that the containers take up much less space than the equivalent number of bottles, and you can always taste wine sold this way before buying. Beware of white wine sold en Vrac, however, as this is much less robust than red and will almost inevitably go off before you have a chance to drink it.

WHAT STYLE?

The basic style of a wine is usually described in terms of colour, sweetness and body or weight. There are other less obvious factors which are also important and affect the style. These include acidity, tannin, fruit character and alcohol. Different styles of wine may be more or less appropriate for different occasions, but it is important also to recognize one's own preferences. You don't have to have white wine with fish just because that is what is usually recommended. People who are often adventurous with food seem to feel constrained by form when choosing wine to go with it.

Colour

Red wine is wine made from red grapes whose skins are left in contact with the rest of the juice during the fermentation process. Apart from the colour which may range from garnet to black, red wines will generally have more body and a stronger flavour than white or rosé. They also contain tannin which comes from the grape skins and is entirely absent from white wines. Tannin is a preservative and so red wines are more suitable for aging, and may take on an interesting extra complexity as a result. Red wines are nearly always dry.

White wine may be made from red or white grapes, but the skins are removed so that there is no contact with the juice during fermentation. The colour varies from almost transparent to golden. The weight of white wine, although less than red wine, can vary quite considerably from very light to something which will stand up to the most strongly flavoured food. Perhaps the most important characteristic of white wines which needs to be considered is the sweetness. They may range from bone-dry to very sweet.

Rosé wines fall between red and white in style, but are generally somewhat nearer to white. They are made from red grapes, and although there are different methods of production, the general effect is of some skin contact with the fermenting juice. The colour ranges from salmon pink to orange. Like white wines they may vary in degree of sweetness, but are rarely sweeter than medium. They are usually drunk in similar circumstances to white wines although they do have extra body.

Apart from the effect it has on the style, depth of colour is often an indication of quality, and is something to be appreciated in its own right when enjoying a wine. As wine gets older, the colour changes. This is most noticeable in red and rosé wines whose colour fades to a tawny shade or even brown. The effect of age is most easily seen by tilting the glass, and looking at the difference between the core and the rim of the wine.

Sweetness

Sweetness in wines is the result of natural sugars which are left at the end of the fermentation process. Red wines are nearly always dry, but white and rosé vary considerably in sweetness, ranging from dry to off-dry to medium-dry to medium-sweet to sweet. Dry wines go best with savoury dishes, and sweet wines go well with desserts. The ones in-between are good to drink on there own or as aperitifs. There are exceptions to these rules however, and the most important thing to consider is one's own preferences.

Body

Body is what gives a wine a certain feel of weight in the mouth. It is important not only when matching a wine with food, or occasion, but also when considering one's own taste. Some people naturally prefer lighter-bodied wines which slip down more easily, whereas others prefer something more robust and substantial. It is one of the most important things to consider when choosing a wine.

Acidity

Acidity is often regarded as something detrimental or negative. A comment that a wine is acidic is generally taken to mean vinegary and unpalatable. In fact acidity is essential and wine would be almost undrinkable without it. Acidity is what gives a wine its refreshing mouth-watering quality, like a glass of freshly squeezed fruit juice. Of course a wine can have too much acidity, giving a jaw-aching, tongue-stinging effect, and it must be balanced with fruit and flavour. Without it, however, a wine has a flabby, soupy quality, and lacks structure and definition. Indeed most of the better wines including Champagnes, Burgundies and Bordeaux are high in acidity. It is also an important preservative, so that it is something to look for in a wine which is to be laid down. The general rule about acidity is that it is higher in wines from cooler climates, and lower in wines from warmer areas. If your geography is sound, this can be a helpful clue as to the style of a wine.

Tannin

Tannin is extracted from the skins of the grapes and is therefore only present in red wines. It is the same as the tannin that occurs in tea and has a similar gum- drying effect when drunk. It can make a wine harsh and undrinkable in large quantities but, if accompanied by plenty of fruit and acidity, tannin indicates aging potential of the wine as it is a preservative whose astringency softens with age. Like acidity, tannin helps to give a wine some structure or 'grip'. It is always present to some degree in red wine and it is a matter of taste as to how tannic a wine should be. It is a bit like how milky you like your tea. People who like a lot of milk in tea are less likely to appreciate tannic wine.

Fruit Character

Pear drops, vanilla, chocolate, tobacco, meat, honey, cheese, wet wool, straw, toast, boiled sweets, the list is endless. It is important not to be intimidated or feel inadequate about flowery descriptions. If you don't get freshly mown grass off Sauvignon Blanc you don't need to get too depressed. Coming up with colourful adjectives can be good fun but it is not essential to deciding what wine you like and actually enjoying it. The important distinctions to make are between general styles of wine.

The age of a wine is important when looking at the character. Young wines tend to show more primary fruit characteristics, that is they show the flavours and aromas of the grapes themselves. Older wines may show more secondary characteristics, that is the effect of chemical changes which take place when the wine is stored in barrel or bottle. These secondary characteristics are the ones which are given the more outlandish descriptions, chocolate, tarmac, tobacco box and so on. They make a wine more complex, and therefore more interesting and appealing.

Another major factor in the character of the wine is the use of oak as a storage vessel at some stage of the fermentation. Oak flavour is imparted into the wine and gives it a good deal more complexity. This is especially the case if it is new oak. Oak can give a wine vanilla, spice or tobacco flavours or aromas.

A large part of the appreciation of a good wine is enjoying the bouquet, and it is here that a lot of the character of the wine is most clearly expressed.

Alcohol

Finally this is maybe the most important ingredient of all. Apart from specially made low-alcohol or non-alcoholic versions, wine ranges from about 8% to 15% alcohol. This is quite a difference and so it is important to check what it says about the alcohol percentage on the label. All drinks sold in the EC must state the level of alcohol on the bottle. In practice most wine will be between 11% and 13%. The degree of alcohol will certainly affect the price of the wine and a naturally high level of alcohol is often considered to be a sign of quality.

Alcohol content also affects the taste of a wine. High alcohol has a warming effect at the back of the throat, and this may or may not be desired. Wines of higher alcohol also get you drunk more quickly, but you probably know that already. The rule with alcohol is the opposite of that for acidity: wines from warmer climates produce higher levels of alcohol.

WHAT OCCASION?

Wine with Food

People can get terribly precious about matching wine with food or occasion, but in reality there are very few rules. As far as food goes, the basic rule is that you don't want to lose the flavour or body of good wine in strong-flavoured food; or delicate food tastes in strong- flavoured wine. (The converse of this rule is also true, that you may want to try and hide the flavour of the food or the wine.) You want to match the weight and flavour of the wine with the strength of flavour of the food. White wines tend to be lighter bodied and are generally considered to be better accompanying delicate flavours. Reds being fuller bodied go better with stronger flavours such as meat and cheese. But it is important to think in terms of the body of the wine rather than the colour when matching.

High acidity is an advantage when matching a wine with very rich food, because it helps digestion. If there is cream in the sauces or a lot of oil, acidic wine helps to cut through and makes its presence felt; it also keeps the palate fresh. Sweetness in food also needs to be matched by sweetness in the wine. If the wine is not sweet enough for the food, its taste will disappear completely.

It is worth remembering that when tasting a wine you should think about the food you may be eating with it. Thus, wine that may seem full-bodied or slightly high in tannins or acid when drunk alone may go very well with food, or light wine that is fine on its own may lose its taste under the flavour of food.

Finally, it is quite a good idea to match the quality of the wine to the occasion. It might be a bit of a pity to waste fine wine on an ordinary meal. Good food deserves good wine and vice versa. Of course people's ideas of how much to spend for special occasions or everyday drinking will differ, but it is important to establish one's own scale so you can start making comparisons.

Wine for Parties

When working out the quantity to buy for a party you need to calculate six glasses to a bottle. Actually working out the amount people are going to drink is extremely difficult, but it is worth thinking about what time of day the party is, how long you are expecting people to stay and whether there will be food.

If you want to offer guests Champagne or other top-quality sparkling wine and are worried about the expense, it is worth remembering that after a few glasses people are much less discriminating. This is not only due to the alcohol, but also to the wearing effect of the bubbles on the palate. It may sound calculating, but it is really very sensible to have a second batch of cheaper stuff for when the best is exhausted. The difference will hardly be noticed.

It is usually a good idea to play safe when it comes to actually choosing the wine to serve. Since some people will only drink white and others only red, it is necessary to provide both. For a staple party drink which is to be drunk without food you don't want anything too full-bodied; light- to medium-bodied reds and some dry and maybe medium-dry white or rosé wines are best.

White and rosé wines are best drunk chilled and this combined with their lightness make them suitable as aperitifs. Bubbles also seem to lighten a wine, and this makes sparkling wine good for summer drinking and aperitifs. Kir, that is still or sparkling wine mixed with a small amount of Crème de Cassis, makes a pleasant aperitif or party drink. It is not worth using expensive wine for this, since much of the flavour of the wine will be lost. This also makes it an economical solution.

TO DRINK NOW OR TO KEEP?

There is a popular misconception that all wine keeps improving with age. Many wines do improve with age, developing subtleties and becoming more complex in character. There is a maximum cellar-life for all wine, however, and much is at its best when purchased and should not be kept very long at all. In general terms: the fuller the body, the more suitable a wine is to keep. Wines for laying down also need to be of good quality, i.e. have enough fruit, acidity and tannin to enable them to develop in the bottle. If the wine is light bodied or of everyday quality it probably shouldn't be kept for more than a year or two. If you are interested in buying more expensive and serious wines from regions such as Bordeaux and Burgundy then check on vintage charts how long the wine should be kept.

The quality of wine from a given vintage (the year the grapes are harvested, which is on the label) varies to a greater or lesser extent depending on the region. The more consistent the climate of the region is the less important the vintage will be. It is a mistake to become too obsessed with vintages. Many experts argue amongst themselves over what is and what isn't a great year. Ratings for vintages are usually given across a large region, and there may be significant local variations; growers who got their timing right in bad years, or growers who had disasters in better years. Poor vintages can also produce very good value wines, simply because there is much less demand for them.

However, it can be worth looking for good vintages of wines with lesser reputations and checking the vintages of top-quality wines to make sure that you are getting good value.

THE WINE LISTINGS

Chapters 2-12 will go through the various wine regions and give an indication of how the wines produced there fit the various styles and categories described above. These descriptions should be of some use when choosing wine, but there is no substitute for tasting. Taste at every opportunity so that you get an idea of what style of wine you like, and don't be influenced by what other people say, or what you are supposed to like.

The main wines that are on sale in the area covered by this book are presented like this:

NAME (Type)

Style:
Price:
Rating:

Comment and description

* **Name** refers to the general descriptive name of the wine. This will include an indication of the quality of the wine. Thus for French wine it could be 'AC Chablis' or 'VDP d'Oc'. The terms 'AC' and 'VDP' are described in Chapter 2.
* **Type** refers to the colour and sweetness of the wine. In ascending order of sweetness, the terms used are **dry**, **off-dry**, **medium-dry**, **medium-sweet** and **sweet**. It is assumed, unless otherwise stated, that the red wines listed are dry.
* **Style** refers to the weight or body of the wine.
* **Price** is described as Low (under £2.50), Mid (£2.50 to £7.50) or High (above £7.50).
* **Rating** gives an indication of whether the wine is generally good value on the other side of the Channel compared to its UK price.
* **Comment and description** gives more information about the wine.

CHAPTER 2

Wine Regions: France

Most of the wine you find in French and Belgian shops is French. There are differences in labelling regulations in the different regions, but the basic classification is the same throughout the country.

There are two categories of table wine: Vin de Table and Vin de Pays; and two categories of quality wine: VDQS (Vin de Qualité Supérieur) and AC or AOC (Appellation d'Origine Controlée). The label of any French wine must state clearly to which of these categories the wine belongs.

Vins de Table may be produced anywhere in the country and are often blends of different wines. They are usually very cheap and can be extremely drinkable but quality is unreliable. It is essential to taste them first before buying in any significant quantity.

Vins de Pays are table wines but with distinct regional characteristics. The label will state the area the wine comes from and may also specify a grape type. There are much stricter quality controls on Vins de Pays than for Vins de Table and, although cheap, quality can be very good. Many Vins de Pays are produced in the South of France in areas not traditionally associated with the production of fine wine. The use of varietal labelling (specifying the grape variety on the label) often reflects a modern approach to wine-making. It is certainly helpful to the consumer as it gives a good indication of the style of a wine. The styles of particular grape varieties are described in Appendix 3.

VDQS is the first category of quality wines. The controls are again stricter than for Vins de Pays. It is quite a small category and most producers of VDQS wines are desperate for them to be promoted to AC so they can command higher prices. Consequently they often work very hard to produce good wines at very reasonable prices.

AC or **AOC** (Appellation d'Origine Controlée) is the top category with the strictest controls. These wines are subjected to a tasting test to ensure they satisfy the requirements, so there is a certain guarantee of quality. If you don't have the opportunity to taste the wine before buying and you do not know the producer you would be safest always to buy AC wine. Wines are often eligible for various ACs; the region as a whole such as Bordeaux, a district within the region such as Haut-Médoc, and a commune within the district such as Pauillac. The more specific the AC, i.e. the smaller the area, the higher the status of the AC. Thus AC Pauillac is higher status than AC Bordeaux. This does not necessarily mean an individual Pauillac wine will always be better than a Bordeaux. It is a bit like the divisions in the football league. A first division club should be better than one from the second or third, but this is not always the case. Tasting the wine will give the definitive answer.

BORDEAUX

Bordeaux produces some of the best and most expensive red and sweet white wine in the world. It also produces some very good red and white wine at very reasonable prices. Buying Bordeaux can be quite confusing because there are a plethora of châteaux and the name Bordeaux may not appear on the bottle at all. Rather than trying to remember all the châteaux names it is best to look at the AC, which will give a good indication of style. The major ACs which come from Bordeaux are listed below. Bordeaux wines are all sold in the traditional tall straight bottles, although nowadays many other wines are sold in similar bottles, so this bottle-shape is not a guarantee that the wine does indeed come from Bordeaux.

In the UK the name Claret is used to refer to red wine from Bordeaux, but this is extremely unlikely to appear on labels on bottles sold in France or Belgium.

Vintage

Vintage is important because the climate is quite variable in the Bordeaux region. The better the quality of wine, the more important it is. Good recent vintages for both sweet white and red wines were '85, '86, '88, '89 and '90. Vintage is less important for dry white wines in Bordeaux which are usually made to drink young.

Classification

The classification system in Bordeaux is not all that helpful. In 1855 the best wines were put into five different categories of **Grand Cru Classé**. However, this was very much biased to the wines of the Haut Médoc region and the categories are very static and slow to respond to changes in quality. There are currently five wines in the highest category: Château Lafite, Château Latour, Château Mouton-Rothschild, Château Margaux and Château Haut Brion. Basically anything that says Grand Cru Classé on it will be extremely good, although not necessarily justifying the price. To confuse matters, certain wines such as Château Pétrus, which is arguably the best wine in Bordeaux, come from regions not included in the Grand Cru Classé classification. Beware of St-Emilion with **Grand Cru** status as this has little guarantee of quality.

Cru Bourgeois is a category to look out for. This is the name attached to wines produced by members of an association of châteaux whose wines are of good quality without being too expensive.

Styles

Red Bordeaux are made predominantly from a combination of Cabernet Sauvignon, Cabernet Franc and Merlot grapes. When Cabernet Sauvignon predominates, as in the Haut-Médoc, the wines are long-living, have powerful blackcurrant fruit flavour and strong character and definition. Those with more Merlot as typified by St-Emilion, are softer, warmer, easier to drink and reach maturity more quickly. Good red wines from Bordeaux are enhanced by the added flavours and aromas from oak-ageing.

The dry whites come from Sauvignon Blanc and Sémillon grapes, which give them a balance of refreshing green fruit and softer floral flavours. Typical of this style are Entre-Deux-Mers.

Some of these too will be stored in oak which makes them a little richer and spicier in character. It can be quite difficult to tell from the bottle whether a wine has been oak-aged, although it will sometimes say **Élevé en Fûts de Chêne**. The sweet whites are made from the same combination of grapes as the dry whites, but with the Sémillon shrivelled by Botrytis, otherwise known as 'noble rot'. This rot turns them into something akin to raisins which ferment naturally into very sweet wine capable of amazingly rich and complex flavours. The best-known name for wines of this type is Sauternes, and the most famous Sauternes is Chateau Yquem, which can fetch hundreds of pounds per bottle.

AC BARSAC   (Sweet White)

Style:	Full bodied
Price:	Mid to High
Rating:	Not noticeably cheaper than in UK

Barsac wines also have the right to the Sauternes appellation and have a similar rich sweet apricot character, but are slightly lighter in style. It is best to look out for those sold under 'Barsac' without a château name, as they are usually cheaper.

AC BORDEAUX/BORDEAUX SUPÉRIEUR   (Red)

Style:	Medium to full bodied
Price:	Low to Mid
Rating:	Great bargains to be found

These wines can range from the elegant fruity Cabernet Sauvignon style to the richer smoother Merlot style. They are quite often blends from different properties and vintages, which will mean they have less character but may well be softer and easier to drink. Sold under this AC the wines should be ready for drinking immediately although they may improve for a couple of years. Bordeaux Supérieur will have slightly more alcohol than AC Bordeaux but little difference otherwise.

AC BORDEAUX   (Dry White)

Style: Light to medium bodied
Price: Low
Rating: Definitely worth buying

Typical dry Bordeaux style made with Sémillon and Sauvignon Blanc, which can be deliciously fruity and refreshing. Quality can be variable though, so it's worth tasting before buying.

AC BORDEAUX CLAIRET   (Dry Rosé)

Style: Full bodied
Price: Low
Rating: Good value

Full bodied for a Rosé, Clairets are like a lighter version of Bordeaux red. This is quite an unusual style, but slips down very easily. It is the sort of wine that is more expensive and much harder to find in the UK.

AC CADILLAC   (Sweet White)

Style: Full bodied
Price: Low to Mid
Rating: Good value

Same grapes as Sauternes produce wine of similar style, but without the complexity or greatness. They can be excellent value dessert wines.

AC CANON-FRONSAC (Red)

Style:	Medium to full bodied
Price:	Mid
Rating:	One to look out for

Exciting appellation not really 'discovered' yet. These wines are similar in style to St-Emilion, soft and grapey and easy to drink. The Merlot grape predominates, and so they are ready to drink quite young; a couple of years after the vintage. Usually very good value.

AC CÉRONS (Sweet White)

Style:	Full bodied
Price:	Mid
Rating:	Cheaper than in UK

Sweet white wine, Sauternes-style but a bit lighter. Generally inexpensive they still show good body and complexity. Good value.

AC CÔTES DE BOURG (Red)

Style:	Medium bodied
Price:	Low to Mid
Rating:	Definitely one to look out for

Excellent value medium-bodied red wines with Merlot grape predominating. The better ones show good smooth, velvety character and plenty of blackcurranty fruit. They can be drunk fairly young, but generally improve for several years in the bottle.

CÔTES DE CASTILLON   (Red)

Style: Medium bodied
Price: Low to Mid
Rating: Can be great value

An excellent St-Emilion style wine, only much cheaper. The name is not as yet terribly well known and there are bargains galore to be had. The quality is not entirely consistent however. Look out for Château Monbadon and Château Pitray which are excellent.

AC CÔTES-DE-FRANCS   (Red)

Style: Medium Bodied
Price: Mid
Rating: Fantastic value

Also with Merlot dominating. Range from lightish-medium to fullish-medium body, similar style to the Côtes de Bourg and also excellent value.

AC ENTRE-DEUX-MERS   (Dry White)

Style: Medium bodied
Price: Low-Mid
Rating: Very Good

In recent years this AC has started producing excellent refreshing dry white wines with plenty of interesting fruity flavours. Can be very good value wines suitable for all occasions.

AC FRONSAC   (Red)

Style: Medium to full bodied
Price: Mid
Rating: Good

Similar style to Canon-Fronsac although maybe not quite as interesting. They still show good characteristics of both Merlot and Cabernet Sauvignon grapes, and are good value medium- to full-bodied red wines.

AC GRAVES   (Red)

Style: Medium to full bodied
Price: Mid to High
Rating: Some bargains to be found

Can produce some of the best and most expensive red wine in the world. They are generally not as robust as wines from the Médoc, but tougher than St-Emilion. Although they err on the expensive side, there is plenty of reasonably-priced stuff which can be very good value.

AC GRAVES   (Dry White)

Style: Medium to full bodied
Price: Mid to High
Rating: Reasonable

Although the white wines used to be very ordinary, they now can be very good fullish-bodied dry wines made to drink within five years of the vintage. They show a good combination of fruit and flowery flavours and are often oaked to give added complexity.

AC GRAVES SUPÉRIEURE   (Sweet White)

Style: Medium bodied
Price: Low
Rating: Likely to be much cheaper than in UK

White wines with slightly more alcohol than ordinary Graves. They are usually sweet wines in the style of Sauternes but not as rich, complex or expensive.

AC HAUT-MÉDOC   (Red)

Style: Medium to full bodied
Price: Mid to High
Rating: Bargains to be found

The classic medium- to full-bodied Bordeaux red wines, with Cabernet Sauvignon dominating. This gives them rich blackcurranty fruit allied with vanilla and spice overtones from ageing in oak. They are usually built to last with a strong backbone of tannin and acidity. Although the best Bordeaux reds are made in this region, the more expensive ones will generally take the more specific AC of one of the six communes in Haut-Médoc; Pauillac, Margaux, St-Julien, St-Estèphe, Listrac and Moulis. Look out especially for Cru Bourgeois.

AC LALANDE DE POMEROL   (Red)

Style: Medium bodied
Price: Mid
Rating: Excellent value, look out for it

A good cheaper alternative version of Pomerol (see below). They are medium bodied, rich and smooth with plummy flavours.

AC LISTRAC (Red)

Style:	Medium bodied
Price:	Mid
Rating:	Not great

These wines are made with Cabernet Sauvignon predominating. They can be quite harsh and the least interesting of the Haut-Médoc wines.

AC LOUPIAC (Sweet White)

Style:	Medium bodied
Price:	Low to Mid
Rating:	Good value

A sweet white wine. Similar in style to Sauternes, but lacking the fullness of body, the richness and complexity of flavour.

AC MARGAUX (Red)

Style:	Full bodied
Price:	High
Rating:	Probably cheaper in the UK

Wonderful, fine, complex Cabernet Sauvignon-dominated wines.

AC MÉDOC (Red)

Style:	Medium bodied
Price:	Low to Mid
Rating:	Well worth checking out

A very large AC, which contains Haut-Médoc. They are medium bodied and similar to Haut-Médoc in style, but more of a mixed bag and generally cheaper. Some Cru Bourgeois have the Médoc AC. These are definitely worth buying.

AC MONTAGNE-ST-EMILION (Red)

Style: Medium bodied
Price: Mid
Rating: Not particularly good value

Along with Puisseguin-St-Emilion, St-Georges-St-Emilion and Lussac-St-Emilion these make medium-bodied easy drinking red wines. They are satellites around St-Emilion and have a similar mix of grapes. They can be good with rich flavours, but are not all that cheap.

AC MOULIS (Red)

Style: Full bodied
Price: Mid to High
Rating: Not likely to be much cheaper than in UK

Moulis produces full-bodied red wines showing typical Haut-Médoc style. They are quite powerful and usually need a few years to soften. They are not the cheapest wines, but can represent very good value.

AC PAUILLAC (Red)

Style: Full bodied
Price: High
Rating: Cheaper in UK

Big blackcurrant flavours from the Cabernet Sauvignon grape, these wines are kept in oak for up to two years to give them tobacco and spicy overtones. They will improve with age over a long period. Unfortunately they are fairly expensive and won't be any cheaper than in the UK.

AC PESSAC-LEOGNAN   (Red)

Style:	Full bodied
Price:	High
Rating:	No cheaper than in UK

These are full-bodied Cabernet Sauvignon-based red wines. The AC falls within Graves and probably contains the best sites and consequently the most expensive wines.

AC PESSAC-LEOGNAN   (Dry White)

Style:	Full bodied
Price:	Mid to High
Rating:	Not significantly cheaper than in UK

Like Graves, but maybe a little higher quality, these wines have delicious fruity flavours and are often oak-aged.

AC POMEROL   (Red)

Style:	Medium bodied
Price:	High
Rating:	No big savings

One of the great ACs for red wines. The Merlot grape is at its best here, producing soft, warm, plummy medium-bodied wines. The wines can age many years, but are usually ready to be enjoyed a few years after the vintage. They are very high quality wines, and generally very expensive. The Belgians love Pomerol and, although no cheaper, you will probably get a better choice in Belgium and France than in the UK.

AC PREMIÈRES CÔTES DE BLAYE
(Red)

Style:	Medium bodied
Price:	Mid
Rating:	Many bargains to be found

Very good value medium-bodied reds, generally at the lower end of the Mid price range, they show characteristic Merlot qualities which makes them more similar in style to St-Emilion than wines of Médoc. They are good value wines ready to drink after three to four years.

AC PREMIÈRES CÔTES DE BLAYE
(Dry White)

Style:	Light bodied
Price:	Mid
Rating:	Good value

These are dry, light-bodied, fruity Sauvignon-Blanc character white wines at fairly reasonable prices.

AC PREMIÈRES CÔTES DE BORDEAUX
(Red)

Style:	Medium bodied
Price:	Low-Mid
Rating:	Very good value

Medium-bodied red wines which are a step up from AC Bordeaux. They usually show the soft fruitiness characteristic of Merlot and are ready to drink fairly young.

AC PREMIÈRES CÔTES DE BORDEAUX
(Sweet White)

Style: Light bodied
Price: Low to Mid
Rating: Well worth seeking out

Straightforward and simple sweet white wines without much complexity. They can serve as good cheap pudding wines.

AC ST-CROIX-DU-MONT   (Sweet White)

Style: Full bodied
Price: Mid
Rating: Excellent value

If your budget doesn't stretch to Sauternes, here's your cheaper alternative. Probably the best sweet white wine in the region after Sauternes and Barsac.

AC ST-EMILION   (Red)

Style: Medium bodied
Price: Mid to High
Rating: Bargains around but need searching out

The classic Merlot-dominated wine, well balanced with Cabernet Franc. Although it is a medium-bodied red wine, the combination of grape varieties give it lightness and make it immediately appealing. The quality of St-Emilions is quite variable though and many are overpriced.

AC ST-ESTÈPHE (Red)

Style:	Full bodied
Price:	High
Rating:	No cheaper than in UK

These are powerful, tannic, full-bodied, oaked red wines. They are typical of the Haut-Médoc style. Unfortunately they are expensive.

AC ST-JULIEN (Red)

Style:	Medium to full bodied
Price:	High
Rating:	Not much cheaper than in UK

St-Julien are also fairly typical red wines from the Haut-Médoc. They are lighter bodied than some of the rest, but still produce good body and rich blackcurrant fruit flavours. You are unlikely to find bargains, but look out for Cru Bourgeois.

AC SAUTERNES (Sweet White)

Style:	Full bodied
Price:	High
Rating:	No cheaper than UK

The greatest sweet white wines in the world. If there was ever a wine to let your descriptives run wild, this is it. The best ones have an intense richness of honeyed, apricoty fruit, with vanilla and spicey overtones. The richness is cut through with a refreshing acidity coming from the Sauvignon Blanc grapes. They get better and better with age. Choose a worthy pudding, Foie Gras or Roquefort cheese to accompany them.

CHAPTER 3

Wine Regions: Burgundy

Burgundy (Bourgogne in French) vies with Bordeaux to be the world's greatest wine region. At best both its red and dry white wines have an amazing combination of full-bodied power and strength combined with captivating subtlety and delicacy of flavour. It is an area which has lived off its reputation, however, and many Burgundies are both poor quality and horribly over-priced. As with Bordeaux, the wines may well not have the name Burgundy anywhere on the label; there are many different ACs across the region, and it is these names which appear. A clue that you are buying Burgundy comes from the traditional tapering neck-shaped bottle, which all Burgundy is sold in.

In Burgundy it is important to distinguish between the AC and the producer. The label will state both names; the AC will be the prominent name on the label and the producer's name will be in smaller writing underneath. Unlike Bordeaux, where a châteaux produces wines from grapes it has grown itself, in Burgundy Négociants (wine merchants) buy up grapes from different small growers throughout the area and make several wines under dif-ferent AC names. The effect of this is that Burgundies often reflect more the style of the producer than the style of a particular AC. Thus, as a general rule, the name of the producer gives a far more reliable indication of the quality of the wine than the name of the AC. Some top producers whose names are worth looking out for are Faiveley, Chanson, Drouhin, Jadot, Latour and Jaffelin; other good producers of slightly cheaper wines are Bouchard Père et Fils, Mommessin and Moillard.

Vintage

As with Bordeaux, vintage is very important for good quality Burgundy. This is particularly the case with the more expensive wines which are made for ageing. Good recent vintages in Burgundy have been: '86 (whites only), '88, '89, '90, '92.

Classification

The classification in Burgundy is less structured and organized than in Bordeaux. The best vineyards are classified as **Grand Cru.** The best wines will be given the appellation of the vineyard such as Le Chambertin, Le Corton and Echézeaux, and are always expensive. **Premier Cru** wines, which are next in the order of merit will have a village name such as Beaune, followed by a vineyard name like Les Epenottes. Premier Cru wines, particularly those of smaller, less prestigious ACs are not always all that expensive and can represent very good value. Other wines will just have a village name or a generic name like AC Bourgogne.

One other sign of quality to look out for is the **Tastevinage** label. The best wines each year are voluntarily submitted to a tasting. Wines showing great merit relative to their AC are accorded this honour.

Styles

The two main red grapes used are Pinot Noir and Gamay. The Burgundies made from Pinot Noir are medium-bodied wines with a delicious strawberry fruitiness which combines with great depth of character. The complexity is enhanced with the added overtones from oak as the wine ages. The less prestigious Burgundies are made from Gamay. This grape has a very approachable light fruitiness, as typified by Beaujolais. These wines from Gamay grapes are less serious than wines from Pinot Noir, and are made to be drunk young.

The best white Burgundy is made from Chardonnay, a grape which produces wines ranging from medium through to full bodied. The character can vary quite a lot, particularly if the wine has been stored in wood, when it takes on a rich butteriness. When unoaked the butter character is still present, but the wine has a fresher fruit flavour. White Burgundy has a more subtle character than Chardonnays from Australia, New Zealand or the USA.

The other white wine grape allowed is the Aligoté. This produces quite acidic inexpensive wines which were originally intended to be mixed with Crème de Cassis to make an aperitif called Kir. All Burgundy made from Aligoté must specify the name of the grape on the bottle.

AC BOURGOGNE   (Dry White)

Style:	Light to medium bodied
Price:	Low to Mid
Rating:	Much cheaper than in UK

As with red, variations in style and quality reflect the producer and area of production. At their best they can show the quality and character of more prestigious Burgundy ACs, at worst they can be light and uninteresting.

AC BOURGOGNE   (Red)

Style:	Medium bodied
Price:	Low to Mid
Rating:	Can be excellent value

Huge variations in style and quality, but these wines made from the Pinot Noir grape are generally on the lighter side of medium with soft fruit flavours. It is worth tasting a few because bargains are definitely there to be found.

AC BOURGOGNE ALIGOTÉ   (Dry White)

Style:	Light bodied
Price:	Low
Rating:	Much cheaper than UK

Cheap, can be a bit thin but good refreshing light bodied wines are also produced. The high acidity of the Aligoté grape makes the wines ideal for mixing with crème liqueurs to make Kir.

AC BOURGOGNE GRAND ORDINAIRE
(Red)

Style:	Light to medium bodied
Price:	Low
Rating:	Much cheaper than in UK

These are fairly light wines made from the Gamay and Pinot Noir grape. Although they can be very cheap they are probably less reliable than AC Bourgogne.

AC BOURGOGNE PASSE-TOUT-GRAINS   **(Red)**

Style:	Light to medium bodied
Price:	Low
Rating:	Very good value

An unusual mix of Gamay and Pinot Noir grapes, making a very easy-drinking approachable fruity wine. It is always cheap, and makes a very good alternative to Beaujolais.

AC CHABLIS   **(Dry White)**

Style:	Medium to full bodied
Price:	Mid to High
Rating:	Look out for cheaper ones

Chablis produces some of the best bone-dry white wines in the world. Unfortunately their reputation is widely known and producers have tended to cash in on the name. Consequently many are overpriced. The more expensive ones tend to be oak-aged, giving them more buttery richness and complexity and greater ageing potential. The cheaper ones are likely to be crisper and fresher and ready for early drinking.

CÔTE CHALONNAISE   (Red)

Style: Low to medium bodied
Price: Mid
Rating: Good value, worth looking out for

AC Givry, AC Mercurey and AC Rully; these are of the lighter, softer, fruitier Pinot Noir style. Givry is likely to be lighter bodied than the other two. They are quite hard to find in the UK, so well worth bringing back.

CÔTE CHALONNAISE   (Dry White)

Style: Medium bodied
Price: Mid
Rating: Great value, often hard to find in UK

These wines go under the names AC Givry, AC Mercurey, AC Montagny and AC Rully. They are lighter than the typical white Burgundy style, but will range from the rich buttery, oaked wines to crisp and refreshing ones. They can be delicious wines, and are well worth buying.

AC [CÔTE DE BEAUNE VILLAGE OR VINEYARD NAME] (Red)

Style: Medium bodied
Price: Mid to High
Rating: Bargains are hard to come by

These can be wonderful red wines, a little lighter in style than those from the Côte de Nuits. They have delicious, light berried fruit flavours allied to great richness and style. Unfortunately they are expensive, with many being seriously overpriced. Some of the names that you are likely to see are: Aloxe-Corton, Auxey-Duresses, Beaune, Ladoix, Meursault, Monthélie, Montrachet, Pommard, Puligny-Montrachet, Santenay, Savigny-lès-Beaune, St-Aubin and Volnay. Many of the same names will appear with different villages or vineyards added on. It is probably better as a rule to go for a good producer rather than a specific AC itself. Villages from which you may find less expensive wines are: Santenay, Savigny-lès-Beaune and Aloxe-Corton.

AC [CÔTE DE BEAUNE VILLAGE OR VINEYARD NAME] (Dry White)

Style: Full bodied
Price: High
Rating: Expensive everywhere

These are the best dry white wines in the world. Unfortunately they are the most expensive. Names you will see are: Auxey-Duresses, Chassagne-Montrachet, Corton-Charlemagne, Meursault, Puligny-Montrachet and St-Aubin. Of these, St-Aubin and Auxey-Duresses are likeliest to be more reasonably priced.

AC CÔTE DE BEAUNE-VILLAGES   (Red)

Style: Medium bodied
Price: Mid to High
Rating: Can be reasonable value

Along with Côte de Beaune these, while usually much cheaper than ACs from single villages, may still be quite pricey. Fairly typical Pinot Noir Burgundy style.

AC [CÔTE DE NUITS VILLAGE OR VINEYARD NAME]   (Red)

Style: Medium to full bodied
Price: High
Rating: Few bargains

These are generally even more expensive than Côte de Beaune. They are typical Burgundy Pinot Noir, but if anything slightly bigger and meatier in style than Côte de Beaune. Again it is hard to find value for money without serious investment. It is very important to look for good producers. ACs include: Chambertin, Chambolle-Musigny, Clos de Vougeot, Echézeaux, Fixin, Gevrey-Chambertin, La Romanée, Marsannay, Morey-St-Denis, Nuits-St-Georges, Richebourg, Vosne-Romanée and Vougeot. Many of these same names will appear with different villages or vineyards added on. Of these, Fixin is likely to be relatively cheap. Marsannay produces very good value wine, but usually lighter in style than the rest.

AC CÔTE DE NUITS-VILLAGES   (Red)

Style: Medium bodied
Price: Mid
Rating: Some good buys available

These are wines made from a select few villages in the Côte de Nuits area. They can produce excellent wines showing the strawberry/raspberry fruit flavours of the Pinot Noir, enhanced by the effects of oak.

AC HAUTES-CÔTE DE BEAUNE (Red)

Style: Medium bodied
Price: Mid
Rating: Definitely worth buying

As with Hautes-Côte de Nuits which are cheaper versions of Côte de Nuits, these are a good cheaper alternative to more expensive Beaune wines.

AC HAUTES-CÔTE DE NUITS (Red)

Style: Medium bodied
Price: Mid
Rating: One to look out for

A very good cheaper alternative to the more expensive red Burgundies. Similar in style to Côte de Nuits-Villages, these wines can show all the better regional and grape varietal characteristics, and produce some of the best value reds in Burgundy. They are seen much less frequently in the UK.

AC MÂCON (Red)

Style: Light bodied
Price: Low
Rating: Mixed quality

Light Beaujolais-type wine, but often a bit more acidic and less fruity. Can be pretty nasty, but good value wines are available.

AC MÂCON/MÂCON-VILLAGES
(Dry White)

Style:	Medium bodied
Price:	Low to Mid
Rating:	Extremely good value

Crisp, fresh and delicious dry white wines. Mâcon-Villages will be slightly fuller bodied, more complex and more expensive. Other village names may be appended to Mâcon, to give ACs such as Mâcon-Lugny, Mâcon-Fuissé, Mâcon-Loche and Mâcon-Solutré. In theory they should be better-quality wines but in practice they may not be worth the extra cost. In general Mâcon white wines are great value low-cost white wines.

AC MARSANNAY (Dry White)

Style:	Medium bodied
Price:	Mid
Rating:	Good value, worth looking out for

These are unusual in that they are white, and come from the Côte de Nuits. Probably the cheapest single-village white Burgundies, producing a typical white Burgundy style.

AC PETIT CHABLIS (Dry White)

Style:	Medium bodied
Price:	Mid to High
Rating:	Can be very good value

Petit Chablis is a little softer and lighter than Chablis and, although usually considered a lesser wine, it is not particularly cheap. It is capable, however, of producing very good quality at a respectable price. Petit Chablis is not usually oaked.

AC POUILLY-FUISSÉ   (Dry White)

Style: Medium to full bodied
Price: Mid to High
Rating: Hard to find bargains

These wines vary from the Mâcon white style to the fuller, more powerful Côte de Beaune. Pouilly-Loche and Pouilly-Vinzelles are similar to the lighter, crisper, fresher style of Pouilly-Fuissé. The Pouilly name is well known, and hence the wines tend to be overpriced.

AC ST-VÉRAN   (Dry White)

Style: Medium to full bodied
Price: Mid
Rating: Great buys

These are as good as Pouilly-Fuissé but are much cheaper because they are less well known. They probably represent the best value compromise between quality and price amongst white Burgundies.

VDQS SAUVIGNON-DE-ST-BRIS
(Dry White)

Style: Medium bodied
Price: Mid
Rating: Worth buying in France

More like a Loire wine. Very enjoyable, crisp, green, refreshing Sauvignon Blanc style. Good value.

BEAUJOLAIS

Beaujolais is actually a part of Burgundy even though the wines it produces are different in style. The wines are almost exclusively red, fresh flavoured, fruity and light bodied. They are made with the Gamay grape which produces wines made to be drunk young. Vintage is more important for the single-village-name Beaujolais Cru wines, which will improve with a little bottle age.

AC BEAUJOLAIS/BEAUJOLAIS NOUVEAU (Red)

Style:	Light bodied
Price:	Low to Mid
Rating:	Can be excellent value

The definitive quaffing wine. At its best Beaujolais is light and fruity and slips down very easily. It is made by a method which reduces to a minimum the extraction of tannin from the grapes and enhances fruitiness. It does have a very limited shelf life of not much more than one year. Don't bother if it's older than that. Beaujolais Nouveau (sometimes called Beaujolais Primeur) is the same wine, but produced for very early release. This means that its sharpness and fruitiness are enhanced. It is almost a different drink from other red wines, but can be refreshing and enjoyable. With all Beaujolais it is very important to select with care, because some of them are of very poor quality.

AC BEAUJOLAIS-VILLAGES (Red)

Style:	Light bodied
Price:	Low to Mid
Rating:	Bargains to be had

This slightly fuller and richer version is a little more expensive than ordinary Beaujolais, but often well worth it if you want a slightly more substantial wine which is still easy-drinking and pleasantly fruity.

AC [SINGLE VILLAGE CRU BEAUJOLAIS] (Red)

Style:	Medium bodied
Price:	Mid
Rating:	Good value

There are ten single villages or 'Cru' in Beaujolais which are entitled to their own AC. These are: Brouilly, Chénas, Chiroubles, Côte de Brouilly, Fleurie, Juliénas, Morgon, Moulin-à-Vent, Regnié and St-Amour. They all produce very pleasant full-flavoured, fruity wines. They are very approachable easy-drinking wines which benefit from some ageing but are nevertheless ready to drink after a couple of years. Of these villages, the wines to look out for are those seen least in the UK. They include Chénas, Chiroubles and Juliénas. Moulin-à-Vent and Morgon are perhaps the fullest bodied and potentially longest-living Beaujolais Cru.

AC BEAUJOLAIS (Dry White)

Style:	Light bodied
Price:	Low
Rating:	Great buys to be found

An unusual blend of Chardonnay and Aligoté grapes which produces some light fresh wines and plenty of fruit, and others with more richness and smoothness. Great variations in quality so it's worth hunting around.

AC CÔTEAUX DU LYONNAIS (Red)

Style:	Light bodied
Price:	Low
Rating:	Worth buying in France

A lesser-known AC which produces fairly light wines with typical Gamay fruit character quite similar to Beaujolais.

AC CÔTEAUX DU LYONNAIS
(Dry White)

Style:	Light to medium bodied
Price:	Low
Rating:	Worth looking out for

Cheap, good-value refreshing wines similar to white Beaujolais. Uncommon in the UK, so especially worth buying if you see them in France.

Vin de Pays
Many of the Vins de Pays are produced from the Gamay grape, and these are often cheap and good value and in the Beaujolais style. Look out in particular for Collines Rhodaniennes and Côteaux de l'Ardèche.

CHAPTER 4

Wine Regions: The Loire

The Loire wine region follows the River Loire, which runs from the centre of France to the north and then west before emerging in the Atlantic at Nantes. Climatically it is a northern wine-producing area, which means that the wines naturally have lowish alcohol and high acidity. Although good red wines are produced, the climate is more suited to crisp refreshing white wines and is the natural home of the Chenin Blanc and Sauvignon Blanc grapes which produce the classic examples of this style.

Vintage

Having a northerly location means that the climate of the Loire is never totally reliable for producing wine. In 1991, for example, production was severely hit in many areas by a late spring frost. Although most of the dry white wine is not made to age very long, a lot of sunshine as in the '89 and '90 vintages can mean richer and fuller wines than usual. Vintage is more important for the better-quality red and sweet white wines, and for these '85, '86, '88, '89 and '90, '91 and '92 were all good years.

Labelling

There is no classification system in the Loire, other than the quality grading that exists throughout France, so the labels on bottles are fairly straightforward.

Styles

The Chenin Blanc and the Sauvignon Blanc are the two main white wine grapes in the Loire. Both these grapes have a high level of acidity which produces wines with an appealing freshness. The Sauvignon Blanc has a character of unripe fruit; green apples or gooseberries. The Chenin Blanc has the same refreshing quality, but with a more flowery character. It is used to produce sweet as well as dry white wines.

The red wines are generally on the lighter side of medium bodied. The main grape is Cabernet Franc which is used alone or in combination with its more famous big brother Cabernet Sauvignon. This produces wines which hint at the blackcurrant fruit of the Cabernet Sauvignon but have a stalky aroma, and are generally lighter and more delicate. Other red wines come from the Gamay and have similar light fruity qualities to Beaujolais. Most of the light red wines are excellent chilled. We generally see relatively few red Loire wines in the UK, and certainly not the cheaper ones, so they are well worth looking out for.

AC ANJOU (Red)

Style:	Light to medium bodied
Price:	Low to Mid
Rating:	Very Good

Much more interesting than their white and rosé counterparts, Anjou produces some of the best value Loire red wines. The better ones are made with a combination of Cabernet Franc and Cabernet Sauvignon, producing wines like Bourgueil. They are lively fruity wines usually drunk young, although the best will also age interestingly.

AC ANJOU (Medium-sweet Rosé)

Style:	Light to medium bodied
Price:	Low
Rating:	Not great

Fairly bland one-dimensional wine. Look out instead for Cabernet d'Anjou, which is crisper and has a more interesting fruit character.

AC ANJOU   (Dry to Medium-sweet White)

Style: Light bodied
Price: Low
Rating: Very mixed

Crisp dry wines made with the Chenin Blanc grape, but not the most interesting. These wines are cheap, but are often fairly dull, although good value can be found.

AC BONNEZEAUX   (Sweet White)

Style: Medium to full bodied
Price: High
Rating: Excellent but expensive everywhere

Sweet wine of the highest quality made from Chenin Blanc. They are from the best area of the Coteaux du Layon and are the fullest bodied. They need several years in bottle to reach their peak, but are capable of matching the richness and intensity of Sauternes.

AC BOURGUEIL   (Red)

Style: Medium bodied
Price: Mid
Rating: Very good value

A good example of the Loire red style. The blackcurrant and leafy characteristics of Cabernet Franc show through giving lively wines that are good to be drunk young. Some Bourgueils are aged in oak casks, and this produces wines which will mature and develop well for several years.

AC CABERNET D'ANJOU (Medium-dry Rosé)

Style:	Light to medium bodied
Price:	Low
Rating:	Reasonable value

A more serious version of Rosé d'Anjou, made with Cabernet Franc and Cabernet Sauvignon grapes. Quality can be variable though.

AC CHINON (Red)

Style:	Medium bodied
Price:	Mid
Rating:	Very good value

Similar to Bourgueil with a light grassy blackcurrant style. If you like the easy refreshing style of Loire reds, these are worth looking out for.

AC COTEAUX DU LAYON (Sweet White)

Style:	Medium to full bodied
Price:	Mid
Rating:	Very good value

These are fantastic sweet wines made from Chenin Blanc with honeyed fruit character but loads of acidity to make them fresh and appealing. They are not terribly well-known and are remarkably good value. These wines can be drunk young but they develop very interesting character as they age.

VDQS GROS PLANT (Dry White)

Style:	Light bodied
Price:	Low
Rating:	Very good value

Same style as Muscadet, but cheaper and less reliable. Can be fantastic value, but beware because poor examples are very common. It is probably safer to go for wines marked 'Sur Lie', as they will have a little more body to balance the acidity. Make sure you taste before buying a significant quantity.

VDQS HAUT POITOU (Dry White)

Style:	Medium bodied
Price:	Mid
Rating:	Very good value

These wines are labelled with the grape variety, the Sauvignon Blanc and the Chardonnay being the two main examples. The Sauvignon is particularly worth seeking out as a cheaper alternative to some of the Loire's more established names.

VDP JARDIN DE LA FRANCE (Dry White/Red/Rosé)

Style:	Light to medium bodied
Price:	Low
Rating:	Excellent

Great variety of quaffable dry whites from Chenin Blanc, Chardonnay and Sauvignon Blanc; reds from Gamay and Cabernet Franc; and rosés. They can be extremely good value, but need tasting before buying in large quantity. It is important also to check the grape variety on the label, to get an idea of style of wine.

AC MÉNÉTOU-SALON   (Dry White)

Style:	Medium bodied
Price:	Mid
Rating:	Very good value

The next-door village to Sancerre, producing similar crisp white wine made with the same Sauvignon Blanc grapes, but less well known and therefore much cheaper.

AC MONTLOUIS   (Dry to Sweet White)

Style:	Medium bodied
Price:	Mid
Rating:	Very good value

Quite similar to Vouvray, also made with the Chenin Blanc grape, these wines range from dryish to sweet. They can have pleasant honeyed character and good crisp acidity. They are less well known than Vouvray and probably better value.

AC MUSCADET   (Dry White)

Style:	Light bodied
Price:	Low
Rating:	Good value

These are very light, crisp wines which do not have huge character beyond their refreshing nature. They can be very good value though and serve as a perfect accompaniment for seafood. They have suffered in recent years in comparison with wines from places like Chile and New Zealand but the better wines, particularly those from Sèvre and Maine, are pleasant and reliable. Look out for labels which bear the words 'Sur Lie', as these wines have matured for longer 'on the Lees', and have more body.

AC POUILLY-FUMÉ   (Dry White)

Style: Medium bodied
Price: Mid to High
Rating: Generally expensive

Not to be confused with Pouilly-Fuissé, a completely different wine. This is top-quality Sauvignon Blanc with wonderful green gooseberry aromas and character, but its name is well known and, as a result, if it's a bargain you're after go for one of the others (e.g. Quincy, Reuilly or Ménétou-Salon).

AC QUARTS DE CHAUME   (Sweet White)

Style: Medium to full bodied
Price: Mid to High
Rating: Good value

Slightly lighter-bodied, drier and more expensive wine of similar character to Côteaux du Layon. They have an excellent balance between honeyed sweetness and acidity and are capable of developing fine complexity with age.

AC QUINCY   (Dry White)

Style: Medium bodied
Price: Mid
Rating: Very good

An excellent, cheaper alternative to Sancerre or Pouilly Fumé from a neighbouring village. Has typical character of the Sauvignon Blanc grape: crisp, fresh and bone-dry. Rarely seen in the UK and definitely worth bringing back.

AC REUILLY (Dry White)

Style: Medium bodied
Price: Mid
Rating: Good

Wine produced from Sauvignon Blanc, similar to Quincy but possibly slightly lighter. It comes from the next-door village, and has the same crisp fresh style. Rare in the UK, it is one to impress friends with as a cheaper version of Sancerre.

AC ST-NICOLAS-DE-BOURGUEIL (Red)

Style: Medium bodied
Price: Mid to High
Rating: Good value

The best but most expensive examples of the leafy blackcurrant-flavoured Bourgueil style. They may be slightly richer and fuller bodied than Bourgueil and made to age.

AC SANCERRE (Dry White)

Style: Medium bodied
Price: Mid to High
Rating: Not the best value

Another top-quality Sauvignon Blanc, although slightly more aggressive in style than Pouilly-Fumé. It can be fabulously refreshing and have wonderful flavours, but its well-known name means that better value will be found from Quincy, Reuilly or Ménétou-Salon.

AC SANCERRE (Red and Rosé)

Style:	Light to medium bodied
Price:	Mid to High
Rating:	Not terrific value

A red wine made from the Burgundian grape Pinot Noir, producing somewhat more delicate wines but with similar light strawberry fruit flavours. Some Sancerre Rosé of a similar but even lighter style is produced. They can be excellent, but nothing with the name Sancerre on it comes terribly cheap.

AC SAUMUR (Dry White)

Style:	Light to medium bodied
Price:	Low to Mid
Rating:	Good value available

These wines are more like Vouvray, but again being less well-known they can be better value. The acidity in Saumur white is very pronounced and is not always balanced by sufficient fruit flavour.

AC SAUMUR (Red)

Style:	Medium bodied
Price:	Mid
Rating:	Excellent

Very good quality Loire Cabernet Franc, showing the best fresh light-fruit qualities of the grape. Like Anjou and Bourgueil, it is not over-abundant in the UK, so definitely worth tracking down and bringing back.

AC SAUMUR-CHAMPIGNY (Red)

Style:	Medium to full bodied
Price:	Mid
Rating:	Very Good

The top end of Saumur wines. These are bigger and fuller bodied than Saumur, with more tannin to make wines to be kept which develop and mature interestingly.

AC SAVENNIÈRES (Dry to Medium-dry White)

Style:	Medium bodied
Price:	High
Rating:	Rare and expensive

Very interesting complex spicy wines with pronounced characteristics of the Chenin Blanc.

AC TOURAINE (Red)

Style:	Light to medium bodied
Price:	Low
Rating:	Very good value

These can have different grape varieties. Very good Gamay are produced which have delicious, light, fruity, Beaujolais-type qualities.

AC TOURAINE (Dry White)

Style: Light to medium bodied
Price: Low
Rating: Excellent value

Excellent alternative to some of the more expensive Loire Sauvignon Blancs. Although much cheaper they show good varietal characteristics of fresh zingy acidity and gooseberry flavours. Look out for them.

AC TOURAINE (Dry Rosé)

Style: Light to medium bodied
Price: Low
Rating: Can be good value

These wines are drier and a little more interesting than Rosé d'Anjou and, although unspectacular, can be perfectly respectable quaffing wines for a summer's day.

AC VOUVRAY (Dry to Sweet White)

Style: Light to full bodied
Price: Low to High
Rating: Variable quality and value

Vouvray covers a wide variety of weight and sweetnesses of wine. They can be fairly light and youthful dry wines, or full-bodied oaked sweet wines made to age for many years. Look out for descriptions on the bottles such as Sec (dry), Demi-Sec (medium-dry) or Moelleux (sweet). All Vouvrays share a flowery honey character and a wonderful mouth-watering acidity. This is a great asset in a sweet wine as it prevents it from being sickly and cloying.

CHAPTER 5

Wine Regions: The Rhône

The Rhône district follows the River Rhône from Vienna to Avignon in south-eastern France. The Rhône marks the beginning of the south, and the style of wine changes to reflect the climate. Grapes in the south receive a lot of sunlight which makes them naturally sweet but low in acid. Since fermentation involves converting sugar to alcohol, the wines which are produced tend to be fairly powerful, but with less of the crisp and refreshing effect of acidity. Although this sort of climate is more suited to producing great red wines than whites, great value can be found amongst the white Rhônes.

The area is divided into two parts: the north which generally produces top quality but expensive red wines, and the south which, as well as producing the great Châteauneuf-du-Pape, is an area where bargains can be found.

Vintage
Being further south, the amount of sunshine the grapes will receive is more stable than in other regions. Good cheap wines are produced in the southern Rhône every year. Vintage here is important for the top-quality northern Rhône wines and the Châteauneuf-du-Papes, but is much less important elsewhere in the Rhône. Good recent vintages for the whole of the Rhône have been '85, '86, '88, and '89 and '91 in Châteauneuf-du-Pape.

Labelling
Rhône labels are straightforward in that there are no complicated quality classifications.

Styles

Northern Rhône

The classic north Rhône red style is based on the Syrah grape. This produces very deep-coloured, big-flavoured powerful rich tannic wines. They have loads of fruit character and improve greatly with age. Unfortunately reds from the northern Rhône are keenly sought after and for the most part fetch very high prices. The white wines from the northern Rhône are made with the unusual Viognier grape. This produces full-bodied but elegant wines, high in alcohol with a distinctive peachy character. They are also rare and expensive. As with Burgundy, producers are very important. Three good (though not necessarily cheap) ones to look out for are Guigal, Chapoutier and Jaboulet.

Southern Rhône

The southern Rhône produces spicy, rich warm and robust red wines, which seem to reflect not only the climate, but also the feel of the place and the character of the people. However, they generally do not have the ageing potential of wines from the north, and lack the subtlety and finesse of the best. Châteauneuf-du-Pape is the exception, producing a very varied selection of great red wines. As far as value is concerned you are better off with some of the cheaper but nevertheless excellent lesser-known names: the big and rich Gigondas and Vacqueyras, or the lighter but punchy Côteaux du Tricastin, Côtes du Ventoux and Côtes du Luberon.

The white wines are less well known than the red and, although in the past many were flabby and uninteresting, there is now a new generation of well-made fresh, crisp and fruity wines.

AC CHÂTEAUNEUF-DU-PAPE (Red)

Style:	Full bodied
Price:	Mid to High
Rating:	Bargains difficult to find

The name Châteauneuf-du-Pape does not give away a lot of information because there is such a huge variety in style and quality. They are invariably robust, fruity wines with more complexity and finesse than other southern reds. It is a very well-known and admired name, and consequently bargains will be hard to come by. Some of the top-quality names to look out for are Château Rayas, Châteaux de Beaucastel and Domaine du Vieux Télégraphe.

AC CHÂTEAUNEUF-DU-PAPE (Dry White)

Style:	Full bodied
Price:	Mid to High
Rating:	Generally overpriced

The well-known name has tended to push up the price of these good-quality rich wines. They can be delicious, crisp and aromatic wines but better value can be found elsewhere.

AC CONDRIEU (Dry White)

Style:	Full bodied
Price:	High
Rating:	Expensive

These are very interesting and distinctive full-bodied white wines with a fragrant apricot character. They have a fanatical following amongst a minority of wine lovers which pushes up the price so as to effectively eliminate less serious drinkers. A good one to produce for your more sophisticated friends, but you do have to pay through the nose for it. Other local white wines which are equally not worth buying are Château Grillet and St-Péray.

AC CORNAS   (Red)

Style: Full bodied
Price: Mid to High
Rating: Expensive but worth pursuing

This is probably the cheapest of the really good northern Rhône reds. It is also one of the fullest bodied. If you are keen to buy a really powerful intense-flavoured wine which will improve greatly with a few years' cellaring, then you could do a lot worse than this.

AC CÔTE RÔTIE   (Red)

Style: Full-bodied
Price: Mid to High
Rating: Top quality but expensive

Fantastic full-bodied rich powerful wine from the northern Rhône which perhaps develops more subtlety and complexity than Cornas. It is regarded a lot more highly though, and consequently is more expensive.

AC CÔTEAUX DU TRICASTIN   (Red)

Style: Medium bodied
Price: Low to Mid
Rating: Very good value

Extremely good value mouth-filling southern Rhône wine with a lighter, less-rich style than many others. These are generally wines to drink young. They are definitely worth seeking out as good-value wines to accompany unfussy cooking.

AC CÔTES DU LUBÉRON (Red)

Style:	Medium bodied
Price:	Low to Mid
Rating:	Very good value

Another example of the lighter-style punchy southern Rhône wines. Although these are generally to drink young, a few of the top-quality ones such as Château-Val-Joanis are made to last.

AC CÔTES DU RHÔNE (Red)

Style:	Light to medium bodied
Price:	Low
Rating:	Good value

Huge variety of wines available, ranging from light to medium bodied, good and bad quality. Great bargains exist, but wines will need careful selection. They are generally fruity and approachable quaffing wines to drink young.

AC CÔTES DU RHÔNE/CÔTES DU RHÔNE-VILLAGES (Dry White)

Style:	Medium bodied
Price:	Low
Rating:	Bargains available but taste before buying

Uncommon in the UK, these ACs have only recently started to produce decent crisp, refreshing, fruity wines. As with most other Rhône whites, they are somewhat distinctive, so it is a good idea to check that they are to your taste.

AC CÔTES DU RHÔNE-VILLAGES
(Red)

Style:	Medium bodied
Price:	Low to Mid
Rating:	Very good

Definitely a step up in quality from the ordinary Côtes du Rhône. These wines are more serious and fuller bodied. They are still, however, very attractive and easy-drinking. You may see a village name such as Cairanne or Rasteau appended to the AC name of this wine. This indicates that the wine comes from that one particular village, and is likely to be better quality still.

AC CÔTES DU VENTOUX   (Red)

Style:	Medium bodied
Price:	Low
Rating:	Very good value

These wines are in the lighter style of southern Rhône, but still have loads of flavour and character. They come from the region next door to Châteauneuf-du-Pape. They can be good quality and are much cheaper alternatives.

VOQS CÔTES DU VIVARAIS   (Red)

Style:	Medium bodied
Price:	Low
Rating:	Very good value

Like Côteaux du Tricastin, with the lighter southern Rhône style, Côtes du Vivarais is another great-value fruity, spicy wine. Easily gulpable, with plenty of punch, it accompanies food very well.

AC CROZES-HERMITAGE (Red)

Style:	Medium to full bodied
Price:	Mid
Rating:	Bargains available

At their best they can be as good as Hermitage, full of rich fruit and spicy flavour, but they can also be quite disappointing and lack the intensity of the really good northern Rhône wines.

AC CROZES-HERMITAGE (Dry White)

Style:	Full bodied
Price:	Mid
Rating:	Good value

Pleasant though unspectacular full-bodied fresh and fruity wines.

AC GIGONDAS (Red)

Style:	Full bodied
Price:	Mid
Rating:	Fantastic

Wonderful warm, spicy, soft, easy-drinking wines with plenty of big flavours. You can taste the climate in these wines which are made to go with large helpings of rich country stew. Definitely worth pursuing.

AC HERMITAGE (Red)

Style:	Full bodied
Price:	High
Rating:	Top quality but expensive

These archetypal northern Rhône wines can rank with the best. As far as price and value are concerned, however, you are probably better off going for something less ambitious.

AC LIRAC   (Red)

Style: Medium to full bodied
Price: Mid
Rating: Very good

Lirac is a less well known neighbour of Châteauneuf-du-Pape, and can also produce a typical full-bodied spicy southern Rhône style. This is another wine to go well with beef stew, and another wine to look out for.

AC LIRAC   (Rosé)

Style: Medium bodied
Price: Mid
Rating: Very good

Fresh and fruity, very enjoyable summer-party, easy-drinking rosé wine. It has good body and is a little more serious than many other rosés.

AC MUSCAT DE BEAUMES-DE-VENISE
(Sweet White)

Style: Full bodied
Price: Mid to High
Rating: Not many bargains

This grapey, sweet and alcoholic wine is the 'Death By Chocolate' of the wine list. Very popular, but some would say it lacks the acidity of Sauternes and Loire whites. Nowadays there are quite a few other interesting and cheaper sweet whites to choose from.

AC RASTEAU   (Sweet Red/White/Rosé)

Style: Full bodied
Price: Mid
Rating: Not great

A cheaper version of Beaumes-de-Venise. Better sweet whites are available. Sweet red and rosé wines are also produced, along with a tawny and a rancio which is a sort of rancid version.

AC ST-JOSEPH   (Red)

Style: Full bodied
Price: Mid
Rating: One to look out for

A bargain, in as much as a wine from the northern Rhône can be a bargain. Can have all the richness, depth and character of Hermitage or Côte Rôtie without being as long-living, serious or expensive.

AC TAVEL   (Rosé)

Style   Full bodied
Price: Mid
Rating: Reasonable

These rosé wines are surprisingly full bodied. They are quite strong flavoured and alcoholic, but lack finesse. They are more suited to having with a full plate of food than on summery occasions in marquees with boaters and light frocks. They also have a tendency to age prematurely and become quite unpleasant.

AC VACQUEYRAS (Red)

Style:	Full bodied
Price:	Mid
Rating:	Very good

Similar in style, but not quite as reliable as Gigondas. Good rich wines worth looking out for.

Vin de Pays
Some good Vin de Pays is produced in and around the Rhône region in a similar style to some of the AC wines. Look out for Vaucluse, Côteaux des Baronnies and Collines Rhodaniennes which produce good, cheap, medium-bodied red wine

CHAPTER 6

Wine Regions: Alsace

Alsace is a region in the north-east of France which produces a variety of styles of mainly dry white wine. Alsace wines are underrated in the UK because they are often mistaken for German wines which have a poor reputation with many consumers. Furthermore, Alsace wines are not particularly cheap, so even lovers of German wines have been put off. In fact the wines are often excellent quality and very good value.

The area Alsace-Lorraine has changed hands between France and Germany several times in the last few centuries and the German influence in the area is still strong. A bottle of Alsatian wine looks German: a tall green flute shaped bottle, gothic script and Germanic names for the grape types. However, the wines are usually fermented dry, have a full body and flavour and are as strong in alcohol content as the best French wine. Alsace wine in the UK tends to be quite expensive; we get mainly the better-quality stuff, but there is an abundance of good, reasonably priced wine available on the other side of the Channel which is definitely worth seeking out.

Vintage
Being fairly far to the north, vintage is quite important in Alsace for the better-quality wines. Good recent vintages have been '83, '86, '88, '89, '90, '91 and '92.

Labelling
Although on first sight Alsace labels can look intimidating they are really quite simple. The three things to look for are: grape

variety, producer and the AC. Grape variety is nearly always stated on the label and this makes life easier than with many other French regions. The varieties are discussed below under styles. The ACs in Alsace are nice and simple, which is another relief. The first is the basic **AC Alsace** which covers most wines in the region. **AC Alsace Grand Cru** is restricted to wine from the best vineyards.

Other descriptions seen on Alsace wine are **Vendange Tardive** which means the wine is made from grapes which are harvested late and therefore have more sweetness in them. The wine produced will be richer, fuller bodied and often with some residual sweetness. **Selection des Grains Nobles** indicates that the wine is made with individually selected hand-picked berries shrivelled by rot (as in Sauternes), producing sweet dessert wines. Both Selection des Grains Nobles and Vendange Tardive wines tend to be expensive and probably not particularly good value compared to the UK.

As with all wines, the producer is very important. Some good ones to look out for are: Sparr, Trimbach, Hugel, Blanck and Zind Humbrecht. Other producers who make good quality but cheaper wine are: Cave Coopérative de Ribeauville, Cave Vinicole de Turckheim, Cave Vinicole de Pfaffenheim, Wolfberger and Scherer.

Styles
The wines of Alsace are generally full flavoured and are made to reflect clearly the grape varietal they are made from. They are usually dry but rarely bone-dry, and they often have an interesting and distinctive spiciness. This makes them fairly different in style from wines of other regions, so you should sample first to see if you like them.

AUXERROIS   (Dry White)

Style: Light to medium bodied
Price: Low
Rating: Very good

Auxerrois was rarely seen as the grape type on Alsace labels, but is becoming increasingly common. It is the main grape in the Edelzwicker blend, and is also used to fill out wines labelled Pinot Blanc. It can produce pleasant if somewhat neutral wines, but its unfashionable name means it is likely to ensure that they are very good value.

EDELZWICKER   (Dry White)

Style: Light to medium bodied
Price: Low
Rating: Very good

One of the few Alsace wines to be made from a mixture of grapes. There is a great deal of variation between different producers, but at their best these can be slightly spicy, interesting wines. A good cheap introduction to Alsace.

GEWÜRZTRAMINER   (Off-dry White)

Style: Medium to full bodied
Price: Mid to High
Rating: Cheaper ones can be good value

This is the Alsace wine par excellence. The flavour and smell are very distinctive, usually described as resembling lychees, and these wines have an unusual spiciness. They are dry but their strong flavour can easily overpower delicate food flavours. They can make a delicious aperitif.

MUSCAT D'ALSACE   (Off-dry White)

Style:	Light to medium bodied
Price:	Mid
Rating:	Good value

Muscat is a very distinctive Alsatian wine which typically has a very grapey aroma and flavour, and pronounced acidity. With the exception of Vendange Tardive wines, Muscat d'Alsace is dry to off-dry. This gives it quite an unusual style because wines from other regions made from the Muscat grape tend to be sweet. Reasonably priced wines are usually available so it is well worth trying it out and bringing some back.

PINOT BLANC   (Off-dry White)

Style:	Medium bodied
Price:	Low to Mid
Rating:	Good value

Apart from Sylvaner, Pinot Blanc is perhaps the grape with the least spicy Alsatian character to it. It can nevertheless have good ripe flavours and pleasant freshness. It is not unlike Chardonnay in its adaptability. Pinot Blancs are generally good value and a good bet as a reliable white wine.

PINOT GRIS   (Off-dry White)

Style:	Medium bodied
Price:	Mid to High
Rating:	Often cheaper than in the UK

Pinot Gris, often called Tokay or Tokay Pinot Gris, is a more lightly spiced wine than Gewürztraminer and can have a lovely creaminess to its texture. It ages extremely well and produces very fine, sweeter Vendange Tardive and Selection des Grains Nobles wines. This is a wine that won't be cheap, but it is not over-abundant in Britain, and is certainly worth discovering.

PINOT NOIR   (Red)

Style:	Light bodied
Price:	Mid to High
Rating:	Good

Pinot Noir is the one red grape grown in Alsace. The wines produced are quite light in colour and, although less substantial than those of Burgundy, Pinot Noir from Alsace are nevertheless well-flavoured wines which can have great character. They have a strawberry fruity style when young, but are also capable of ageing. This is not the cheapest of red wines, but they will generally be a little better value than in Britain and more choice is available.

RIESLING   (Dry White)

Style:	Medium bodied
Price:	Mid to High
Rating:	The cheaper ones are worth buying

Riesling is the most 'noble' of Alsace wines. The wines made to drink young will be the best value; they are delicious, refreshing wines with good fruit and body. As they age they become very serious, capable of matching the best from anywhere. There are fantastic examples of Vendange Tardive and Selection des Grains Nobles.

SYLVANER   (Dry White)

Style:	Medium bodied
Price:	Low to Mid
Rating:	Very good

Sylvaner has a fairly low status in Alsace and it is certainly true that it doesn't have the potential for greatness of the likes of Riesling or Pinot Gris. It does, however, produce reliably good refreshing wines with characteristic Alsace spiciness which slip down very easily. These wines are low priced, and made to be drunk fairly young.

Others

Although not in Alsace, other wines of interest from eastern France are:

AC ARBOIS VIN JAUNE (Off-dry White)

Style: Full bodied
Price: Mid to High
Rating: An interesting novelty

This is a very unusual, intense-flavoured sherry-like wine, which has to be tasted to be understood. There is also a sweet wine from this region called Vin de Paille, which has an intense apricot and nutty flavour and is made from dried grapes.

AC SAVOIE (Dry White)

Style: Medium bodied
Price: Mid
Rating: Reasonable

Fairly rich medium-bodied complex wines often made with Chardonnay grapes.

CHAPTER 7

French Country Wines

Country wine is the name given to wines from vineyards outside the classic French wine regions. Since these wines have a lower reputation than others from more famous places, they can be extremely good value. Many country wines are seen much less often in Britain, so they are good ones to bring back to enhance one's reputation as a wine connoisseur.

THE SOUTH-WEST

The wines from the south-west are made with similar grapes and in a similar style to Bordeaux. But, unlike Bordeaux, there is no hierarchy of classification so labelling is much clearer and buying the wine is more straightforward. Vintage is less important than in Bordeaux because, being further south, the weather is more consistent and generally the wines are of lesser quality and not produced to be aged for long periods. Apart from the normal French system of AC, VDQS, VDP and Vin de Table there is no special classification for wines from the south west.

This area is not regarded as one of France's top wine-producing regions, and is certainly considered greatly inferior to neighbouring Bordeaux. Many good cheap wines are produced here, however, and lack of reputation is always good news from a consumer's point of view because it means that prices are reasonable. However, with a proliferation of ACs and VDPs, quality is often inconsistent, so it is a good idea to taste before buying a large quantity.

AC BERGERAC   (Red)

Style: Light to medium bodied
Price: Low to Mid
Rating: Very good

Cheaper less-reknowned versions of Bordeaux reds which are extremely good value, and well worth looking out for. There are some excellent full-bodied rosés around too.

AC BERGERAC SEC   (Dry White)

Style: Light bodied
Price: Low
Rating: Very good

Like Bordeaux whites although lighter, these are a delicious combination of the refreshing Sauvignon Blanc and flowery Sémillon grapes. Bergerac whites can be excellent value. Taste before buying though.

AC CAHORS   (Red)

Style: Full bodied
Price: Low to Mid
Rating: Very good value

Generally big flavoured, rich and tannic, made with the Malbec grape with some Merlot mixed in. Very good with substantial meaty meals. Definitely worth buying if you enjoy the style.

VDP COMTÉ TOLOSAN (Red)

Style: Medium bodied
Price: Low
Rating: Very good value

Another wine that you rarely see in Britain, but Comté Tolosan can produce very good, straightforward Bordeaux-type red wines. These wines use similar grapes to Bordeaux but are not made to be kept long.

AC CÔTES DE BUZET (Red)

Style: Medium bodied
Price: Low to Mid
Rating: Very good

These are wines made with Cabernet grapes in the Haut-Médoc Bordeaux style. They can be extremely good and available at very reasonable prices. Many of the wines are oak-aged.

AC CÔTES DE DURAS (Red)

Style: Light to medium bodied
Price: Low
Rating: Excellent

Delicious light versions of red Bordeaux, with the Merlot grape predominating, at extremely good value.

AC CÔTES DE DURAS (Dry White)

Style: Light to medium bodied
Price: Low
Rating: Very good

Good everyday drinking, dry white wine in the Bordeaux style. Very good value.

VDP CÔTES DE GASCOGNE (Dry White)

Style:	Light to medium bodied
Price:	Low
Rating:	Very good

Very popular now in the UK, this wine is very reliable. The label may not impress your friends, but it is unlikely to let you down with its ease of drinking and its fresh fruitiness.

AC CÔTES DU FRONTONNAIS (Red)

Style:	Medium bodied
Price:	Low
Rating:	Mixed but can be very good

These wines, which are rarely seen in the UK, are fairly full bodied, rich and fruity. They are made from a mixture of Bordeaux and southern French grape varieties for early drinking, and are well worth trying.

AC CÔTES DU MARMANDAIS (Red)

Style:	Medium bodied
Price:	Low
Rating:	Very good

Good imitation slightly lighter versions of Bordeaux reds.

AC GAILLAC (Red)

Weight:	Light bodied
Price:	Low
Rating:	Good value

Gaillac are light-bodied fruity wines made in the Beaujolais style which can be delicious. There is also a Gaillac Primeur, equivalent of Beaujolais Nouveau.

AC GAILLAC (Dry White)

Style: Light bodied
Price: Low
Rating: Very good

Quite similar to Bordeaux white wines, perhaps with a little more exotic fruit flavour.

VDP GERS (Dry White)

Style: Light to medium bodied
Price: Low
Rating: Extremely good

Very cheap easy-drinking white wine with similar character to Côtes de Gascogne. Not a special occasion wine, but slips down nicely all the same.

AC JURANÇON (Medium-dry White)

Style: Medium Bodied
Price: Low to Mid
Rating: Unusual but can be good value

This is an unusual medium-dry wine with spicy and tropical fruit flavours. If you like the style of Alsace wines, particularly Gewürztraminer, this one might interest you. They improve with age.

AC JURANÇON SEC (Dry White)

Style: Light to medium bodied
Price: Mid
Rating: Unusual, not cheap

An unusual wine similar in character to Jurançon. This wine is better drunk young however.

AC MADIRAN   (Red)

Style: Medium to full bodied
Price: Low to Mid
Rating: Good

These are powerful tannic wines which can have great style. They are built to age, but never seem to soften up completely. Can be very good value.

AC MONBAZILLAC   (Sweet White)

Style: Medium bodied
Price: Low to Mid
Rating: Excellent

Can be the perfect cheaper version of Sauternes. Made with the same grape varieties but not having quite the same intensity of flavours. Another excellent wine from the same area is AC Saussignac, which includes Chenin Blanc in its mix and has a more citrussy character. Both these make great dessert wines at a reasonable price.

AC PACHERENC DU VIC BILH   (Dry to Medium-dry White)

Style: Medium bodied
Price: Mid
Rating: Good

An unusual wine with exotic fruit and floral flavours, which can be excellent. It comes in various degrees of sweetness, so check carefully before buying.

AC PÉCHARMANT   (Red)

Style:	Medium to full bodied
Price:	Low to Mid
Rating:	Excellent

Pécharmant produce the best-quality, fullest bodied wines in Bergerac. They can be excellent value, much cheaper versions of Bordeaux. Look out for them.

THE SOUTH-EAST

Wines from the south-east are produced from a combination of Rhône grapes: Syrah, Cinsault, Grenache, Mourvedre and Carignan and, to a lesser extent, the Bordeaux grapes Cabernet Sauvignon and Merlot. The reds tend to be quite straightforward, fairly full bodied, rich and spicy. They are usually very good companions to meaty dishes. A lot of rosé is produced in Provence which may be fairly full flavoured (for rosé), but nevertheless good summer glugging wine.

As with the south-west, there is no special classification of wines, and vintage is not over-important because the weather is fairly consistent and most of the wines are made to be drunk fairly young anyway.

AC BANDOL   (Red, Rosé)

Style:	Full bodied
Price:	Mid to High
Rating:	Reasonable value

Bandol produces excellent big tannic red wines capable of rich fruit flavours which develop interestingly after a few years in bottle. Unfortunately they command high prices in the Côte d'Azur where they are grown, and are therefore not particularly good value.

Bandol also produces fairly powerful good-quality rosés which are cheaper and better value than the reds.

AC BANYULS (Sweet Red/Rosé/Tawny/White)

Style:	Medium to full bodied
Price:	Low to Mid
Rating:	Good value

These are rich, sweet fortified wines which are high in alcohol and have great concentration. Look out for the Grand Cru, which have been aged in oak and have more defined and interesting combinations of spicy and nutty flavours.

VDP BOUCHES DU RHÔNE (Red)

Style:	Medium to full bodied
Price:	Low
Rating:	Good value

A variety of Bordeaux and Rhône grapes produce full bodied warm southern red wines. None too subtle, but straightforward and good value.

VDQS CABARDÈS (Red)

Style:	Medium bodied
Price:	Low
Rating:	Good value

Medium- to full-bodied wines made with southern Rhône grapes, giving plenty of fruit and character. Rarely seen in Britain.

AC LA CLAPE (Dry White/Red/Rosé)

Style:	Full bodied
Price:	Low
Rating:	Excellent value

Red, white and rosé wines from La Clape are all full-bodied southern style wines, which soften and improve greatly with age. Unusual and rarely seen in UK, so worth looking out for.

AC CORBIÈRES (Dry White)

Style:	Light bodied
Price:	Low
Rating:	Good value

A pleasant easy-drinking fresh and slightly spicy wine without an enormous amount of character. Good for informal occassions.

AC CORBIÈRES (Red)

Style:	Medium to full bodied
Price:	Low to Mid
Rating:	Very good

Ranges from simple, robust and cheap barbecue wines to excellent quality complex oak-aged wines. They all have a richness and warmth that is evocative of the south.

AC COSTIÈRES DE NÎMES (Red, Rosé)

Style:	Medium bodied
Price:	Low
Rating:	Very good value

These are simple light- to medium-bodied fruity wines with some spicy character. They are inexpensive and worth seeking out. Excellent value rosé is also produced here.

AC CÔTEAUX D'AIX-EN-PROVENCE
(Red, Rosé)

Style: Full bodied
Price: Low to Mid
Rating: Very good

Full-bodied red wines made from typical southern grapes: often mixed in with Cabernet Sauvignon. The result is a rich fruity wine which has elegance. They are definitely worth picking up. The rosés produced here are also particularly good, fairly light in body, have plenty of fruit and are not usually terribly expensive.

AC CÔTEAUX DU LANGUEDOC   (Red)

Style: Medium bodied
Price: Low
Rating: Very good

Consistent good value plonk.

AC CÔTES DE PROVENCE   (Red,Rosé)

Style: Full bodied
Price: Low to Mid
Rating: Good

Huge variation of wine styles and qualities in this large appellation. The reds are generally good, full-bodied wines with plenty of southern warmth. Some are made for early drinking and others for ageing a little. The rosés are cheap and reasonable without being outstanding.

AC CÔTES DU ROUSSILLON (Red)

Style: Medium bodied
Price: Low to Mid
Rating: Good

Another southern red in the same mould; plenty of fruit and a little spice to match. A slight step up in quality is the Côtes du Roussillon Villages, which is likely to be a little more expensive.

AC FAUGÈRES (Red)

Style: Full bodied
Price: Low
Rating: Very good

Another one for the barbecue or the beef stew, with its warm, spicy southern style. These wines are consistent and underrated.

AC FITOU (Red)

Style: Medium bodied
Price: Low
Rating: Good

Popular in Britain, so no one will be terribly impressed with the label, but none the less these are excellent value, rustic, fruity red wines.

AC MINERVOIS   (Red)

Style: Medium or full bodied
Price: Low to Mid
Rating: Good

These wines are generally good value full-bodied, warm and
spicy southern wines. Beware, however, because as with other
southern reds they can be a little rough. Minervois is sometimes
made in a softer lighter style but unfortunately it is not possible
to work this out from the label.

AC MUSCAT DE ST-JEAN-DE-MINERVOIS   (Sweet White/Rosé)

Style: Medium Bodied
Price: Low
Rating: Very good value

An excellent alternative to Beaumes-de-Venise. St-Jean-De-
Minnervois has the same rich grapey flavours but is much better
value.

AC RIVESALTES   (Sweet White/Rosé/Tawny/Red)

Style: Medium bodied
Price: Low to Mid
Rating: Good value

These are fortified sweet wines often much better value than others which are better known. They are rich, alcoholic and port-like
in style. AC Muscat de Rivesaltes is similar, but has a more
grapey flavour. If you enjoy sweet fortified wines these are definitely worth trying.

AC ST-CHINIAN   (Red)

Style:	Light bodied
Price:	Low
Rating:	Excellent

Similar mix of grapes and style to Côtes du Rhône, these wines are light-bodied, easy-drinking and excellent value.

VIN DE PAYS

In recent years there has been a proliferation of Vins de Pays areas created in Provence and Languedoc-Roussillon, and many wines are now produced under this classification. There is variation in quality and style but there is also a fair degree of similarity. Most of the wine is red, and medium to full bodied. The grapes used are the typical 'southern' grapes: Carignan, Cinsault, Grenache, Mourvedre and Syrah along with the likes of Cabernet Sauvignon and Merlot from Bordeaux. The wines generally have plenty of rich fruit flavour and some spiciness but an approachability that makes them easy to drink and immediately appealing. Many are labelled with the grape type, which gives a good indication of style.

Some of the better wines of this style which are low priced are: Aude, Catalan, Côteaux de la Cité de Carcassone, Côtes de Thongue, Gard, Herault, Île de Beauté (from Corsica), Mont Bouquet, Oc, Pyrenées-Orientales, Sables du Golfe du Lion, Vallée du Paradis and Var.

Some good, cheap rosés with clean, fresh flavours fuller in body than many from elsewhere come from: Ardèche, Aude, Oc, Sables du Golfe du Lion (often sold as Listel) and Var. Look out for Vins de Pays sold in bag in the boxes. This can be an extremely cheap way of buying pleasant quaffing wine.

CHAPTER 8

Wines from Italy, Spain and Portugal

ITALY

Italy stretches a great distance from the Alps in the north to north Africa in the south, and encompasses a huge range of climates, terrains, grape varieties and hence wine styles. In wine terms, Italy has everything from the woeful to the wonderful. There is not that much Italian wine on sale in France; the best selection being at shops aimed at visiting Brits. Belgian supermarkets normally sell a reasonable range. Since Italian producers tend to be able to get a good price at home for their better-quality wines, these are not generally exported at bargain prices. However, many cheaper Italian wines are available at considerable savings on the continental side of the Channel compared to the UK.

Labelling

Italian wine is classified in a similar way to French wine. The equivalent of the French AC or AOC is **DOC**, which in Italian stands for Denominazione di Origine Controllata. There are controls on grape types, yield and production methods used for these wines, but in practice there is a huge variation in quality between diferent DOCs, and it is probably less reliable an indication of quality than AC is in France. There is a stricter category of **DOCG** (Denominazione di Origine Controllata e Garantita), but although the quality is generally more consistent, it is not a significant step up from DOC.

The next category is **IGT** (Vino da Tavola con Indicazione Geografica). Wines of this status will show 'Vino da Tavola' on the label, but will have a village or region name and possibly a grape type. This is equivalent to French Vins de Pays, and indicates a table wine with certain regional characteristics. It is quite a new category and it is hoped that this will encourage producers of inferior table wine to improve quality. Finally comes basic **Vino da Tavola**, which is made with little control of quality.

A confusing anomaly about Italian wines, however, is that the conditions required for DOC and DOCG often inhibit the creativity of wine producers by banning certain grape varieties and production techniques. To get round this, many producers are making their best wines under table wine classifications where no such restrictions exist. The irony is that Italy's greatest wines are currently classified as Vino Da Tavola.

There are various words worth looking out for on the labels of Italian wine. **Classico** is an indication of wine produced in the heartland, or prime growing area of a DOC region. It is nearly always a sign of good quality. **Riserva** specifies a wine with an extra period of ageing, often in oak barrels. **Amabile** or **Abbocato** means medium sweet.

There are many good Italian producers, but the choice will be very limited. One name that is likely to crop up is **Antinori**, who produce wines of very reliable quality which, in addition, are widely available.

Style
There are many different styles of Italian wine which reflect the variations in climate and soil type. The wines that will be worth buying in the area covered by this book will generally be low-priced, light-bodied and light-flavoured white and red wines. They do not always have a huge amount of character, but are simple, easy drinking and cheap. Two good examples of this are the white wines labelled with the grape varieties: **Pinot Bianco** and **Pinot Grigio**.

DOCG BARBARESCO (Red)

Style: Full bodied
Price: High
Rating: Few bargains

Barbaresco is a slightly lighter, cheaper and more reliable version of the more famous Barolo (see below).

DOC BARDOLINO (Red)

Style: Light bodied
Price: Low to Mid
Rating: Reasonable savings

Similar to Valpolicella (see below), Bardolino is pale, light and refreshing. It has a slight bitterness to it and is best drunk young.

DOCG BAROLO (Red)

Style: Full bodied
Price: High
Rating: Poor

These are wines made for ageing, high in alcohol tannins and acid. They have fairly complex full-blown flavours but are unreliable and expensive. They are probably not worth pursuing on the other side of the Channel. If you do find something that looks worthwhile, check out the vintage, as it is important with Barolo. Good recent years are: '82, '85, '86, '88, '89 and '90.

DOCG CHIANTI   (Red)

Style: Medium bodied
Price: Low to Mid
Rating: Savings on cheaper wines

These wines are light and fresh with red fruit flavours when young, but they mature into a richer and more serious style when the wine has been softened with age. Chianti is often aged in oak, and the flavour reflects this. Quality in Chianti is generally fairly reliable.

DOC FRASCATI   (Dry White)

Style: Light bodied
Price: Low to Mid
Rating: Reasonable savings

Various nuances in character of these pleasant light-bodied mellow-flavoured wines. They have a tendency to be a little bland.

DOC ORVIETO   (Dry or Medium-sweet White)

Style: Medium bodied
Price: Mid
Rating: Small savings

Crisp light-flavoured wines with good body, although they can also be a little bland. The best are from the Classico regions. Quite good sweet wines are also available. These are labelled Abboccato or Amabile.

DOC SOAVE   (Dry White)

Style: Light bodied
Price: Low to Mid
Rating: Good savings

Most Soave is fairly typical light Italian white wine, which is dry and fresh and good for parties. Soave Classico can be a lot more interesting, with a creamy texture and a slightly bitter almondy flavour.

DOC VALPOLICELLA   (Red)

Style   Light to medium bodied
Price: Low to Mid
Rating: Reasonable savings

Very refreshing bright, fruity wine. It has an up-front youthful character that can be delicious. Quality, however, is very variable and Valpolicella can be fairly nasty, so be sure to taste before you buy, unless you see the reassuring Classico on the label. Made to drink young, although you occasionally see the wine labelled Amarone, which is altogether different; a much richer-flavoured and more serious wine.

DOC VERDICCHIO DEI CASTELLI DI JESI   (Dry White)

Style: Light bodied
Price: Low to Mid
Rating: Reasonable savings

Pale light-bodied wine with fresh but slightly neutral flavours. Stands out in its amphora-shaped bottle.

SPAIN

Spain has traditionally been a source of cheap wine. With a few notable exceptions the use of old-fashioned and inefficient wine-making techniques meant that the quality of the wine was fairly poor. This was particularly the case for white wine which needs quite sophisticated temperature-controlling equipment to prevent oxidation in a hot climate. In recent years, however, there has been a sharp improvement in production techniques, so that now there is a much greater variety of Spanish wines that are worth buying. As with other non-French wines, choice is not as good as in the UK. The best choice will again be in British-run shops.

Labelling

Denominacion de Origen or **DO** is the quality category for Spanish wine equivalent to AC in France. Unfortunately the letters DO are not always specified on the label, so it can be difficult to identify quality wine.

As with Italy, some of the better wines are not made under the DO classification at all, because there are restrictions to the grape varieties that may be used. They will then be made as table wines or **Vino de Mesa**.

For quality Spanish wine there will be a small label on the back of the bottle, which gives an indication of how long the wine has been aged. Although the amount of ageing varies between regions, the general rules are that wines labelled **Crianza** have aged for at least two years of which one was in oak barrels. **Reservas** must have aged for three years, with at least one year in oak barrels. **Gran Reservas** must have aged for five years with at least two years in oak barrels. Sometimes you will see Sin Crianza, or an absence of any of the other terms, which will mean that the wine is to be drunk young and has not been oak-aged.

Generally for red Spanish wine a long period of oak-ageing is considered to be a sign of quality. It does also mean that the style will be different from young wine. It will be drier, have flavours of vanilla and spice and less immediate fruitiness. These characteristics may or may not be what you are looking for.

Although the quality of each vintage varies, it is generally less important in Spain than it is in France. It is probably only worth pursuing vintages of the best-quality Spanish wine, and this is unlikely to be worth buying in France or Belgium.

Style
The main wine regions are:

DO LA MANCHA   (Red and Dry White)

Style: Medium bodied
Price: Low
Rating: Can be very good value

Although not entirely reliable, and not a label which will impress your guests, La Mancha wines are often extra cheap, very straightforward and perfectly acceptable.

DO NAVARRA   (Red)

Style: Medium to full bodied
Price: Low to Mid
Rating: Very good value

Excellent cheaper versions of Rioja, which use the same Tempranillo grape. Although difficult to find across the Channel, they are definitely worth seeking out.

DO PENEDÈS   (Red and White)

Style: Medium to full bodied
Price: Mid
Rating: Only small savings on UK prices

The Penedès wines that you see will inevitably be made by the Torres company. They produce excellent wines with plenty of body and flavour, which show good clean characteristics of the grape varieties they are made from. The labels are very clear with information about style and grape varieties. Look out for Vina Sol, Gran Viña Sol and Viña Esmerelda (white), and Sangredetoro and Gran Coronas (red), although savings over UK prices will be fairly small.

DO RIOJA   (Red)

Style: Medium bodied
Price: Low to High
Rating: Good value particularly for cheaper wines

Red Rioja comes in two styles: youthful and fresh with delicious strawberry flavours, or complex and mature with a wonderful vanilla flavour which comes from the ageing process in oak barrels. The quality is very consistent and, while not always cheap, it is usually very good value, particularly for the older style. The grape used is the Tempranillo, and you often see this on labels of wine from other regions producing a similar style to Rioja.

DO RIOJA   (Dry White)

Style: Light to full bodied
Price: Low to High
Rating: Variable

As with Red Rioja, the white comes in the two styles of mature and youthful. You need to check on the back of the bottle how much maturation the wine has undergone. At their best, the youthful wines can be light and fresh, and the oaked wines can be full of unusual spicy character. You are much more likely to encounter the younger style of wine. The mature versions are not particularly good value.

DO VALDEPEÑAS   (Red)

Style: Medium bodied
Price: Low to Mid
Rating: Very good value

Slightly rougher versions of Rioja, these red wines are very good value. Look out for Señorio de Los Llanos.

PORTUGAL

Portugal is usually lumped together as an adjunct to Spain but in reality it produces wines which are very different in style. The climate is much cooler, affected by the Atlantic, and the wines generally reflect this by being more acidic. Many Portuguese wines are distinctive and unusual because they are produced merely for the domestic market and don't take into account more international tastes. They are characterized by high levels of acidity in whites and very tannic reds. There is even a grape variety whose name translates as Dog Strangler, the acidity of the wine produced is so strong it feels like you are being choked. In recent years the Portuguese have become much more export-minded, and many wines are now produced in collaboration with foreign wine makers, and are much more approachable and easy-drinking.

Labelling

DOC (Denominacao de Origem Controlada) denotes a quality wine-producing region and is the equivalent to AC in France. There are currently nine of these regions. In addition there is now a new category of **IPRS** (Indicacoes de Proveniencia Regulamentada) which are probationary DOCs. These regions are not well known outside Portugal but are all trying their best to achieve high quality and their wines are therefore likely to be good value.

Garrafeira is a term that sometimes appears on wine labels. It means that a wine has been aged for a longer time than usual. The actual length will vary from region to region.

The Wines

Although many top-quality wines are produced in Portugal they are not readily available in the vicinity of the Channel Tunnel. These are the styles of wine you are likely to encounter:

DOC BAIRRADA (Red)

Style: Medium to full bodied
Price: Mid
Rating: Limited availability, moderate savings

Bairrada can be very interesting full-bodied, strong-flavoured wines with fairly pronounced acidity and tannins. They can be quite astringent when young, but they age well, producing wines with good rich flavours. Needs fairly substantial food.

DOC DÃO (Red)

Style: Medium bodied
Price: Low to Mid
Rating: Moderate savings

Another Portuguese red wine with strong flavours. They are mixed in quality, but can provide a powerfully flavoured wine at fairly low price.

MATEUS ROSE (Off-dry Rosé)

Style: Light bodied
Price: Mid
Rating: Reasonable savings on UK prices

In between dry and medium-dry in sweetness, Mateus Rosé is a fairly neutral lightly sparkling wine made for drinking chilled on summer days at picnics or parties.

VINHO VERDE   (Dry White)

Style: Light bodied
Price: Low
Rating: Good savings

Vinhos Verdes are mouth-tinglingly refreshing youthful white wines with a slight sparkle. There is not a lot to them otherwise, but their high acidity and low alcohol make them enjoyable swigging wine.

CHAPTER 9

Wines from Germany and Austria

GERMANY

Traditionally, German wine has served a different function to French wine. Whereas in France wine was viewed as an essential accompaniment to food (to complement the taste, and to aid digestion), in Germany wine was viewed as a drink to be had on its own. The style of the wines reflected this difference. French wine was generally dry to accompany savoury food, or sweet to go with dessert. German wine was fruity and medium-dry, designed to have the immediate appeal to enable it to be glugged merrily on its own.

Although the industry has changed significantly in recent years to accommodate the more modern taste for dry wine, the production of medium-dry to sweet white wines is still the norm in Germany. One name stands out, and the reputation - or lack of reputation - of German wine is built mainly upon the fame of Liebfraumilch. Although it is very cheap and easy drinking, it is a mass-produced drink, and quality is often very poor.

Liebfraumilch is the German wine sought by many British people, but there are plenty of other similar fruity medium-dry wines such as Niersteiner Gutes Domtal and Piesporter Michelsberg. In fact most cheap German wine will be like this, so if you like the style, look out for the many cheap alternatives to Liebfraumilch.

German wines can be very good quality, and if you have a

taste for wines with a degree of sweetness balanced by fabulous mouth-watering acidity, they can be well worth pursuing. There are good new dry wines as well. Unfortunately you are unlikely to see much good-quality German wine for sale in France or Belgium.

Labelling

At first sight, German wine labels look very difficult to understand but there are only a few things to look for. These are quality status, place of origin, grape type and vintage.

Quality Status

The first category is **Deutscher Tafelwein**, which is basic, light-bodied sweet wine. **Deutscher Landwein** (usually dry) is a light bodied wine with some regional character. **Qualitätswein (QbA)** is dry or sweet wine from a specified region which is checked for quality. In practice quality is quite variable. Both Landwein and QbA wine are often labelled **Trocken** (dry) or **Halbtrocken** (medium-dry) to indicate how sweet they are.

The highest-quality wine is **Qualitätswein mit Prädikat (QmP)**. There are several categories of QmP wine which refer to the natural sugar level of the grapes before the wine is produced. Of these, **Kabinett** produces dry to medium-dry wine often fairly low in alcohol, **Spätlese** is a little sweeter and higher in alcohol and **Auslese** is sweeter and stronger still. The quality of all these wines can be very good. The other categories of **Beerenauslese**, **Trockenbeerenauslese** and **Eiswein** are all very sweet, expensive and rare. None of them are readily available in the Channel Tunnel area.

Labels will also have a village or vineyard name and a producer's name. These are important on bottles of wine of good quality.

Area of Origin

The famous German wine areas are **Mosel-Saar-Ruwer** and the Rhine (which includes **Rheingau**, **Rheinhessen**, **Rheinpfalz**, and **Nahe**), both of these produce crisp white wines fairly low in alcohol by French standards. Mosel wines are lighter in body and paler in colour than those from the Rhine. Both regions specialize in wines made from the Riesling grape. Other good wine-producing regions are: **Hessische Bergstrasse**, **Württemberg** and **Baden.**

Grape Type

The grape that produces the best German wine is definitely the **Riesling**, whose wines are fabulously refreshing with flowery scents and fruity flavour.

Although wine made from other German grapes such as the **Silvaner**, **Scheurebe**, **Kerner** and **Müller-Thurgau** often are fairly bland, they are capable of very good quality.

Red wine is produced in Germany, but very little is exported.

Vintage

Vintage is not very important for the type of German wine likely to be found in the shops covered in this book.

KABINETT   (Off-dry to Medium-dry White)

Style: Medium bodied
Price: Low to mid
Rating: Can be good value

Not much choice available but Kabinett wines can be delicious, refreshing wines with interesting fruit character and not too sweet. They are generally fairly low in alcohol which makes them excellent as aperitifs.

LANDWEIN   (Dry to Medium-dry White)

Style: Light bodied
Price: Low to Mid
Rating: Good value

Rarely seen but can be good value dryish white wine. Look out for the labelling **Trocken** (dry) and **Halbtrocken** (medium-dry).

LIEBFRAUMILCH   (Medium-sweet White)

Weight:	Light bodied
Price:	Low
Rating:	Big savings possible

Easy-drinking party wines, to drink on their own rather than with food. Simple and straightforward. They start from around 8F (£1), which represents a big percentage saving over the UK. Likely to come in litre bottles and magnums too. Other similar cheap, sweet German party wines to look out for are: Bereich Bernkastel, Deutscher Tafelwein, Niersteiner Gutes Domtal, Piesporter and Michelsberg. It should be noted that all of these can produce wines of reasonable quality, but in general the ones you are likely to see will be cheap and simple.

SPÄTLESE   (Medium-dry White)

Style:	Medium to full bodied
Price:	Low to Mid
Rating:	Can be good value

Again very little choice of these good-quality sweetish wines. The best by far are made from Riesling and come from the Mosel or the Rhine. At their best they have excellent body with rich and complex fruit flavours. They are stronger in alcohol than Kabinett, but fairly weak by French standards.

AUSTRIA

You would expect Austrian wines to be similar to German ones and in many ways they are. There is a quality grading system very similar to the German, with Tafelwein, Landwein, Kabinett and similar QmP categories. In fact the requirements for achieving a quality category are more stringent than the German ones and represent a more reliable indication of quality. Similar grape types are used to Germany, again with the Riesling considered as the most noble variety.

The difference with Germany is a result of the recent modernization of the industry, where producers have moved away from the old-fashioned gothic script image. The wine labels are very readable, with information clearly set out. They always indicate the sweetness of the wine, which is a distinct advantage over German bottles. Austria is now much more export conscious and far more dry wines are being made using familiar grape varieties. Pinot Blanc, Chardonnay and Sauvignon Blanc all produce very respectable wines. Although white predominates, some red wine is also produced from the local variety Blauer Portugieser. This produces a low cost, light-bodied wine low in acidity.

A little Austrian wine is available in Belgium, but next to none in France with the notable exception of the Grape Shop in Boulogne. With Austria's admission to the EC on 1 January 1995, a little more should become available.

By far the most abundant Austrian wines are made from:

GRÜNER VELTLINER (Medium-dry White)

Style:	Medium bodied
Price:	Low to Mid
Rating:	Fairly good value

Wines from this grape are best when young, being crisp and refreshing with an interesting spicy, leafy character.

CHAPTER 10

Wines from Eastern Europe

Although wine has long been produced in eastern Europe, there has been quite a significant increase in production in recent years. The first country to become aware of the foreign currency-earning potential from exporting well made low-cost wine was Bulgaria, but other countries, particularly Slovakia, Hungary and Romania have since joined the band-wagon. The wines are rarely particularly exciting or likely to really stick in the memory, but they are sound in quality and low in cost, making most of them extremely good value.

There are some traditional grapes grown and wine styles produced, but the demand seems to be more for the familiar French varietals - Cabernet Sauvignon, Merlot, Pinot Noir, Chardonnay and Sauvignon Blanc - and these are the ones that you are most likely to see.

The labelling of eastern European wines is fairly straightforward, with the grape variety usually the most prominent name. **Controliran** on Bulgarian wine is an indication of quality control.

Choice of eastern European wines is as yet fairly poor in France, although a few are available in Belgium. The Calais British-run warehouse stores are the places where you get the best choice.

BULGARIA

Bulgaria produces the pick of the red wines from eastern Europe, mainly from Cabernet Sauvignon and Merlot grapes. Unlike wine producers in the New World, the Bulgarians seem intent on producing imitations of French wines.

BULGARIAN   (Red)

Style: Medium bodied
Price: Low
Rating: Significant savings

Bulgaria produces wines from Merlot and Cabernet Sauvignon grapes which are good imitations of basic Bordeaux. Although more reliable, and therefore a safer bet than French wines at an equivalent price, they are less likely to give you a pleasant surprise and set flowery adjectives tripping off the tongue.

BULGARIAN   (White)

Style: Medium bodied
Price: Low
Rating: Good savings available

Bulgarian white wine is less good than the red. Chardonnay and Sauvignon Blanc are the main grapes used but the wines often seem to lack freshness and character. White wines from Hungary and from Slovakia seem to be a better bet.

ROMANIA

PINOT NOIR   (Red)

Style: Light to medium bodied
Price: Low
Rating: Very good

This is an excellent, refreshing light-bodied wine with bags of strawberry flavour. Extremely good value if you can find it.

HUNGARY

HUNGARY (Dry White)

Style: Medium bodied
Price: Low
Rating: Very good

Hungary produces very good, cheap, fresh-flavoured Chardonnays and Sauvignon Blancs. These grapes seem to express slightly different qualities in Hungarian wine, with floral and fragrant characteristics.

TOKAY (Sweet White)

Style: Full bodied
Price: Mid
Rating: Not much cheaper than in UK

Very distinctive strong Hungarian dessert wine, coming in various degrees of sweetness. The wines will age for many years, producing amazing sherry-like aromas and flavours of caramel and vanilla amongst others. The choice is not very good, and prices won't be much cheaper than in Britain.

OTHERS

You may see wines from other eastern European countries, which are usually labelled with grape variety names, and are likely to be cheap and good value. Ones to look out for are: **Moldova**, which produces good **Pinot Noir** and **Slovakia,** where reasonable Sauvignon Blanc and Gewürztraminer are made. **Slovenia** produces the famous medium-sweet neutral-flavoured Lutomer Laski Riesling and some good Chardonnay.

CHAPTER 11

New World Wines

You sometimes get the impression from European wine makers that wine is a mysterious thing; information should not be conveyed in a straightforward way, clearly written on the label, but must be hidden and coded so that only the *cognoscente* can decipher it. The great advantage of buying wine from the New World is that producers there do not adhere to this curious belief. In fact their rather novel marketing idea is that information on the wine label should be as clear as possible. The labels nearly always state the grape varieties used, often they will say whether the wine has been oak-aged and if so for how long. Luckily for us this information is nearly always written in English. If ever you are completely lost and without a clue in a wine shop your best bet is probably to look for the Australian section, because you can be sure that at least there will be plenty of clear information on the label to help you choose.

As yet there isn't much New World wine sold in France. The shops where you are likely to see it are places run by the British or aimed very much at the British. Much of this wine actually arrives via Britain, so the savings will not be huge; just reflecting the differences in duty between Britain and France. These usually amount to between £1 and £2 per bottle.

In Belgium you see a fair bit more New World wine, but the choice still isn't nearly as good as in Britain and savings are really only possible on the cheapest wine.

AUSTRALIA

There are quite major differences between the philosophy of wine-making in Australia as compared with Europe. In Europe, particularly France, the concern is with the land, the 'terroir' or soil. A wine's quality is put down to the uniqueness of the soil and microclimate of where it is grown. The Australians stress the importance of technology and the care and control of the production process once the grapes have been picked. Australian producers pay less attention to wine regions, but concern themselves more with the type of grapes they are using.

The most important thing on an Australian wine label is therefore grape type, with information regarding where they come from being secondary. Indeed it is not unusual for grapes from different vineyards in different areas of the country to be used in the same bottle of wine. The wines below are therefore classified by the grapes which are used.

Wine Style

Australian wines are made to enhance the characteristics of the grape variety they are made from, and this gives the wine prominent and powerful flavours. They are often described as 'up front', which means that they hit you with all they have in the first mouthful without too many hints and overtones lingering in the background. This gives them immediate appeal and makes them very attractive. They are also extremely consistent in quality and very good value.

Vintage

Vintage is less important than in France as the weather is more stable generally, and grapes from different regions are often used to produce a wine. This means that although there will be differences in style from year to year, good wines are produced every year.

Labelling

There is no quality classification system in Australia and wine labels are helpful and straightforward. It is the reputation of the producer that is important when buying the wine. Good producers to look out for are **Penfolds**, **Rosemount**, **Brown Brothers**, **Wolf Blass**, and **Lindemans**.

CABERNET SAUVIGNON (AUS)   (Red)

Style: Full bodied
Price: Mid to High
Rating: Good-quality wine at a reasonable saving

The classic Bordeaux grape made into a wine of great boldness
and fruitiness. The more expensive wines are likely to be more
subtle, and include blends of Merlot and Cabernet Franc grapes.

CHARDONNAY (AUS)   (Dry White)

Style: Medium to full bodied
Price: Mid
Rating: Classic Aus white, a little cheaper than in UK

Very sound approachable wines. Rich ripe fruit very much to the
fore. During maturation, these wines are usually exposed to a lot
of new oak which gives distinctive vanilla and creamy flavours.
Some people consider them to be over-oaked although this is
very much a question of taste.

RHINE RIESLING (AUS)   (Dry White)

Style: Medium bodied
Price: Mid
Rating: A little cheaper than in UK

Rieslings show very prominent fruitiness so that on first tasting
you think they will be sweet, but they are usually dry. These are
good aperitif wines. Riesling is used a lot in the cheaper blends
where no grape type is specified, making them easy-drinking and
appealing.

SAUVIGNON BLANC (AUS)   (Dry White)

Style: Medium bodied
Price: Mid
Rating: A little cheaper than UK

Unlike Loire whites, Australian Sauvignon Blanc are often oaked and rounder in flavour. They are much less zingy and acidic, but still show the familiar, prominent gooseberry flavour.

SÉMILLON (AUS)   (Dry White)

Style: Full bodied
Price: Mid
Rating: Distinctive Australian style

Another grape producing big rich wines which are nearly always oaked. Sémillon has less obvious fruit character than Chardonnay, and is often added to fill Chardonnays out. In wines made from a mix of the two grapes, it is the first name on the label which predominates.

SHIRAZ (AUS)   (Red)

Style: Full bodied
Price: Mid
Rating: Very Australian wine, good value

This is the same grape as the Syrah from the Rhone. It produces very full-bodied, big-flavoured wines with deep dark stewed-fruit character. There is also a peppery quality and spiciness to these wines. Shiraz grapes are often added to Cabernet Sauvignon. The Cabernet gives a bit of structure and definition to the wine, while the Shiraz adds body and flavour.

NEW ZEALAND

New Zealand has a much cooler climate than Australia, and the wines it produces reflect this. They are light to medium in body, and have a crisp and refreshing quality which is due to the higher levels of acidity in the grapes. Good wines are produced from Chardonnay, Cabernet Sauvignon, Merlot and Pinot Noir which show typical varietal characteristics, but are much toned down from their Australian counterparts. It is for **Sauvignon Blanc** however, that New Zealand has acquired a great reputation. These are delicious refreshing wines with incredible flavours of gooseberry and citrus fruit.

The choice of New Zealand wines is very limited in continental Europe and you are only really likely to find major names such as **Cook's**, **Stoneleigh** and **Montana**. They should all be between £1 and £2 cheaper a bottle.

Although characteristics of the wine will vary with the year of vintage, good medium-priced wines are produced each year, and quality in New Zealand is very consistent.

SOUTH AFRICA

The quality of South African wine definitely lagged behind the rest of the New World during the years of economic isolation. The market which the country emerged into was much more competitive, with higher standards of production and fresher, cleaner-tasting wines made from the classic grape varieties. Since 1993, South African wines have come on by leaps and bounds, and they now stand shoulder to shoulder with those from Australia and New Zealand in terms of quality.

The wine industry is much older and more established than in Australia and New Zealand, so as well as the familiar French grapes such as Chardonnay and Cabernet Sauvignon which show typical characteristics, there are some more distinctive and unusual flavours that are worth seeking out in South African wines. **Pinotage** produces soft, rich flavoured red wines, while **Steen** (Chenin Blanc) has soft citrus flavours without the usual high acidity.

There are very few South African wines sold in France. You are likely to see a few cheap examples in Belgium which are fairly good value.

USA

Nearly all the American wine available in France or Belgium will be Californian. These wines concentrate on the classic French grape varieties: Cabernet Sauvignon, Pinot Noir, Chardonnay and Sauvignon Blanc, and their style is somewhere between France and Australia in terms of the boldness and 'up-frontness' of flavours. The Americans make many fine wines but they fetch high prices on the domestic market and are not particularly good value in Europe.

The wines you are likely to see will be fairly cheap wines of reasonable quality made from familiar grape varieties (at smallish discounts on UK prices). The one unusual Californian grape is **Zinfandel** which produces rich blackberry-character wine.

CHILE

Chile produces large quantities of wine made from familiar grape varieties at very reasonable prices. The quality is generally good without being outstanding, and the wines can be marvellous value. The most successful grape in Chile is probably the Cabernet Sauvignon which produces wines with good acidity and plenty of blackcurrant fruit. Chilean wines generally stress the character of the grapes used, without knocking you over the head with flavour as many Australian wines try to do. Aside from Cabernet Sauvignon, good Chilean wine is also produced from Merlot, Sauvignon Blanc, Chardonnay, Riesling and Gewürztraminer.

As with most New World wines, the majority that you see in France will be in shops aimed at British customers. A few more are available in Belgium, but probably with only the cheapest ones much cheaper than in the UK.

OTHERS

Interesting new wines are being produced in Argentina, Brazil and Mexico and you may encounter some of these in the more adventurous shops. The wines which are exported are made from familiar grape varieties and are usually good value.

CHAPTER 12

Sparkling Wines

For some strange reason you pay 60% more duty for sparkling wine than for still wine in the UK. In France, there is minimal difference between the two. This means that the savings to be made on sparkling wine are even bigger than on still wine. Unfortunately the guidelines allow for only 60 litres of sparkling wine to be brought back rather than the 90 litres of still wine so it is worth thinking up a good reason to convince the customs officials to increase your allowance.

The best sparkling wine is made by the Champagne Method or Méthode Champenoise. The bubbles of carbon dioxide are formed as a result of a second fermentation which takes place inside the bottle. The bubbles created in this way are very small and consistent in their regularity, and the wine produced will have a deeper and more interesting character. Another cheaper method which produces wine of lesser quality involves using large tanks where second fermentation takes place under pressure before the wine is bottled. The most basic method involves injecting carbon dioxide into the wine, like with a soda siphon. These are distinctly poorer in quality, and a tell-tale sign of this production method will be the sudden manic rush of large bubbles when the bottle is opened, which then promptly disappear as the wine goes prematurely flat.

Vintage
Many fizzy wines are blended from different varieties and different vintages of grapes, so the year of production of the wine is rarely important. Most champagne is non-vintage (a blend from

different years). A small amount of champagne is released with a vintage year, and this will be high-quality expensive stuff. It is much fuller bodied and richer in flavour than non-vintage style. When choosing a vintage champagne, however, the style of a particular house (producer) is likely to be more important than the actual vintage.

Labelling

Sparkling wines usually fall within the classification system of the country they come from, so expect to see the usual quality terms which are specific to each country: **AC** (France) **DOC** (Italy) **DO** (Spain) and so on. Sparkling wines come in various degrees of sweetness, so look out for the terms: **Brut** (dry) and **Demi-sec** (sweet). Occasionally you see **Extra Brut** (very dry), or **Doux** (very sweet). Although these are French terms, you often see them on wines from other countries.

All champagne is made using the Méthode Champenoise. Other wines made using this method may not use any part of the name 'Champagne' on the label. Instead they may use the term **Méthode Traditionelle**. Another term you may see is **Mousseux** which means sparkling. **Crémant** wines are also sparkling, but with a slightly softer sparkle.

FRANCE

AC BLANQUETTE DE LIMOUX
(Dry White)

Style:	Medium bodied
Price:	Mid
Rating:	Excellent

This is an excellent sparkling wine made by the Méthode Traditionelle, very clean and dry in style and often with plenty of fruit coming through. It can be fairly cheap, and is definitely one to look out for.

AC CHAMPAGNE (Dry to Sweet White/Rosé)

Style: Medium to full bodied
Price: High
Rating: Very good

The greatest sparkling wine in the world, typified by a toasty bis-
cuity character, strong acidity and deceptively full body which
matches up well to food. Rosé champagnes usually taste very
similar to white, although the acidity may be a little softened. The
two basic types are vintage (a year will be written on the label)
which has fuller body and more distinct character, and non-vintage - a blend of wines from different years which will have a certain house style. Reasonable champagne starts at around 65 F in
France and it is at this sort of price that the biggest savings are to
be made. Unfortunately at the low price level it is very difficult to
know what you are getting unless you taste first. You can be
sorely disappointed. For this reason supermarkets are probably
not the best place to buy, because shops are more likely to have
built up a relationship with a tried and tested producer. Look out
for the letters RM on the top of the bottle, which represents a
small grower/producer whose product is likely to be made more
carefully than that of a large cooperative. There are variable savings to be made on Grandes Marques (big name) champagnes.
These can often be well worth buying at supermarkets, so look
out for promotions. In general, vintage champagnes and more
expensive blends are unlikely to be much cheaper than in Britain.

AC CLAIRETTE DE DIE (Dry to Semi-sweet White)

Style: Light to medium bodied
Price: Mid
Rating: Very good value

This is quite a delicate-flavoured sparkling wine with floral characteristics. It comes in various degrees of sweetness, but the style
seems less well suited to the very dry wines. It is at the cheap end
of the Mid-price range and makes a respectable fizz for informal
occasions.

AC CRÉMANT D'ALSACE (Dry White/Rosé)

Style: Medium bodied
Price: Mid
Rating: Good value

Excellent wines with plenty of flavour and character. They are made from a variety of grapes but should show signs of the typical Alsace spice and hint of sweetness.

AC CRÉMANT DE BOURGOGNE (Dry White/Rosé)

Style: Medium bodied
Price: Mid
Rating: Good value

An excellent alternative to champagne, this is one of the nearest in style and quality, having a very similar mix of grapes. The rosé might be particularly attractive, because there is very little reasonably priced pink champagne. Good Crémant de Bourgogne is not the cheapest though, and unfortunately you don't see that much of it in shops and supermarkets in the Calais area.

AC CRÉMANT DE LOIRE (Dry to Semi-sweet White/Rosé)

Style: Light to Medium Bodied
Price: Mid
Rating: Very good value

A huge variety of grapes and styles but quality is consistently good. They generally have quite a soft creamy style with light fruit flavour. Check the label to see what degree of sweetness you are getting.

AC SAUMUR MOUSSEUX   (Dry to medium-sweet White/Rosé)

Style:	Medium bodied
Price:	Mid
Rating:	Very good value

Saumur is the local favourite champagne substitute which is one very good reason for buying it here. The wine is generally fruity with an attractive zippiness. Not the cheapest fizz available, but a distinctive wine, and quality is usually very good.

AC VOUVRAY MOUSSEUX   (Dry to Sweet White)

Style:	Medium to full bodied
Price:	Mid
Rating:	Good value

These are nearest in style to Saumur, being made principally from the same grape (Chenin Blanc), but slightly fuller bodied, with richer honeyed character. It is also a little softer in style, without Saumur's liveliness. Vouvray is a sparkling wine which isn't trying to imitate champagne, and has its own unique character.

OTHER COUNTRIES

ASTI SPUMANTE   (Medium-sweet White)

Style: Light bodied
Price: Low to Mid
Rating: Good savings

Asti Spumante is an uncomplicated sweet grapey style of wine. You will find this in shops aimed at British customers, where good savings can be made on the UK prices. Look out also for the very similar Moscato. Some of these are available for around 10 F, a huge whack cheaper than anything you'll find in Britain.

DO CAVA   (Dry White)

Style: Medium bodied
Price: Mid
Rating: Reasonable savings

Cava is Spanish sparkling wine, with Freixenet Cordon Negro the most famous example. You won't see much in France except at shops and warehouses run by the British, but in Belgium there will be a little more. Cava generally has a broad mouth-filling quality to it with less pronounced acidity than champagne and other sparkling wines.

DOCG LAMBRUSCO   (Dry to Sweet Red/White)

Style: Light bodied
Price: Low
Rating: Big savings

The archetypical light fizzy party wine. They are simple straight-forward wines not to be taken too seriously at prices significantly cheaper than in the UK. You will find them in all the shops aimed at visiting Brits.

NEW WORLD SPARKLING (Dry White/Rosé)

Style:	Medium bodied
Price:	Mid
Rating:	Very good for cheaper ones

These wines generally have a mouth-filling quality and more pro-nounced fruit character than their French counterparts. Although choice is much better back in the UK, the difference in duty means that there are major savings to be made on the cheap New World wines. If you need to buy a cheap sparkling wine without tasting it first, look no further than Seppelt's Great Western pink or white from Australia, which you can pick up for around 22 F from most English-run shops. This represents a saving of 40% on the UK price. You should find familiar names like Mumm Cuvee Napa (US), Lindauer (NZ) and Yellowglen (Aus). These are priced around 40 - 55 F and will be a couple of quid cheaper per bottle than back home. Remember, however, that you can usually get at least 15% case discounts on sparkling wine in Britain, and so savings on cases of these wines may be smaller.

SEKT (Dry to Sweet White)

Style:	Light to medium bodied
Price:	Mid
Rating:	Hardly worth buying

This German sparkling wine usually has some sweetness to it. You won't see much Sekt about and it is probably not worth buy-ing unless you travel to Germany.

CHAPTER 13

Beer and Cider

BEER

The current guidelines for the amount of beer which may be brought back to Britain from another EC country are 110 litres, and with the duty in France about ⅛ of what it is in the UK it doesn't take a brilliant mathematician to work out that huge savings can be made. You can certainly save £1 per litre on familiar brands such as Fosters, Stella and Holsten Pils, and a lot more on local beers.

It is important to note this difference between familiar brands seen in the UK and the local ones. Many of the most popular beers in Britain are not popular in France or Belgium and have to be imported specially for the cross-channel trade. The savings on these beers are generally the duty alone. There are greater savings possible on other beers which are sold locally anyway. These beers are cheaper because the volumes sold are higher and so distribution is more efficient and the pricing more competitive. For example La Strasbourgeoise, a lager of 4.9% abv, can cost the equivalent of about 60p a litre, whereas Grolsch (which is one of the cheapest international brands with an equivalent strength) costs around 95p a litre.

Many of the local brands of lager are just cheaper examples of familiar types of beer. However, one of the joys of buying in France or Belgium is the great variety of unusual beers which are either completely unavailable or very expensive in Britain. One example of this is Belgian beer, but there are also many brews from Flanders, Strasbourg and other areas of northern France which are worth investigating.

PACKAGING

Beer comes in cans and bottles of various sizes in packs of 4, 6, 8 or 24. In addition to the normal 33cl bottle which is most common in Britain, a lot of beer is sold in the small 25cl bottle and larger 50cl and 75cl bottles. The 440cl can is now the standard beer can size for British beer drinkers, but you also see a number of smaller 33cl and 50cl cans in continental shops.

What are the advantages and disadvantages of the different types and sizes of package? If you go to Belgium it is interesting to see how few beers are sold in cans. Just as a serious wine drinker would be horrified at the idea of drinking wine from a can, a Belgian beer drinker will tell you that this is the wrong way to drink beer. It is undeniable that beer does acquire a slightly metallic taste from the can but whether this matters when glugging standard brands of chilled lager is another matter.

You would generally expect beer to be cheaper when sold in larger containers, but this is not the case. The cheapest Stella Artois I saw was 42 F for 24 x 25cl bottles, whereas in cans it cost 96 F for 24 x 50cl cans. This is about 15% more expensive. In addition, many of the cheaper French lagers are only available in 25cl bottles.

The disadvantage of buying small bottles, however, is that they add to the weight and bulk, and space which will probably be at a premium in the back of your car. It can also be a little irritating if you are used to drinking beer by the pint to have to keep returning to the fridge for replacements for the small bottles.

Many French and Belgian beers are sold in 75cl bottles, which are a good size to accompany meals. This is not usually the cheapest way of buying beer, but the pleasing rustic appearance of these bottles, especially with corks and wire cages, can add to an occasion.

There are nearly always discounts for bulk. Packs of 4, 6 and 8 are generally cheaper than singles, and packs of 24 are always cheaper. Many places offer discounts for pallets, but you are talking about seriously large quantities there. Whatever way you buy the beer, take note of the size of container to get a good price comparison. You may well need a calculator if you are intent on getting the best buy.

STRENGTH

When buying beer, it is important to consider the alcoholic strength. Strength must by law be marked on the bottle or can, and will usually appear as abv (alcohol by volume) which is the volume of alcohol as a percentage of the total volume of the beer. It is strength which determines to a large degree the price of beer, so it is essential to check out the strength to get an accurate price comparison.

If you are not sure what to buy, it is well worth considering the strength of the beer. Most of the beers sold in the UK are between 3% and 5%. Ordinary lager is about 3.2%, Export or Pils style lagers are about 5%, whereas Superstrength lagers go up to 8% or 9%. If you are consuming a large quantity, this represents a significant difference in the inebriating effect.

In France and Belgium you see many more strong beers, some go as high as 12% abv which is the strength of wine. Different strengths could be appropriate for different occasions; a stronger beer might be more suitable for accompanying food, whereas weak beer might be more appropriate for downing in large quantity on a hot summer's day. The strength of a beer does also affect the taste; weak beers may lack bite, whereas many but not all overstrength beers may have a sweet malty taste.

STYLE

The difference in beer styles reflects differences in the ingredients used: malts, hops and water. The major determinant, however, is the type of yeast used and the resultant method of fermentation. The two basic methods are 'top fermentation' and 'bottom fermentation'.

Top fermentation occurs at a warm temperature (between 15° and 25°C), the yeasts rise to the top and there is contact with the air. The beers mature over a few days at this temperature and develop more individualistic but less clean styles, with fermentation often continuing in the bottle or cask. The resultant beer is known as **ale** and is drunk at a natural cellar temperature. Bottom fermentation takes place at cooler temperatures (around 9°C). The yeast falls to the bottom, and the whole process is carried out to minimize contact with air. Once fermented, the beer may be matured over a longish period in cool conditions of storage. The beer produced is referred to as **lager** and is normally drunk chilled. Lager tends to be cleaner in style than ale, but usually has less character.

Beer is produced in many different countries, with different characteristics. Those that are most often encountered in France and Belgium are listed below.

BEER TERMS

Some of the terms you might encounter on beer labels are:

Abdij/Abbaye/Abbey	Brewed in similar style to Trappist beer
Abv	Alcohol by volume (the usual measure of alcohol)
Ale	Top-fermented beer
Bière Blonde	Light-coloured lager beer
Bière Brune	Dark lager beer
Bière de Garde	Strong good-quality beer to keep
Bière de Table	Beer low in alcohol, originally intended to accompany food
Bitter	Well-hopped English top-fermented ale
Draught	Nitrogen-capsule mechanism in can which gives the frothy effect of draught beer
Dry	A marketing term which refers to a beer with a distinctive dry finish

Export	Export refers to a premium beer usually a little over 5% abv
Extra	Refers to beer of extra strength alcohol
Ice Beer	Current marketing fad which refers to beers which have been frozen during production to enhance certain flavour characteristics
Lager	Bottom-fermented beer
Lambic	Wheat beer which ferments spontaneously due to wild yeasts
Pils	Premium quality lager beer in style of Czech Pilsener
Porter	Fairly strong, dark stout-like brew made with roasted malts
Stout	A very dark top-fermented beer made with roasted malts
Super	Super strength lager up to 9% abv
Trappist	Special name which refers to five high quality Belgian monastery breweries
Triple	Term used in Belgium to denote the brewery's strongest beer
Wheat Beer	Also called white beer, this refers to a pale sour-flavoured beer made from wheat

INTERNATIONAL

These are the common lager brands seen all over the world with names such as Heineken, Fosters, Budweiser, Stella Artois and Kronenbourg, and will be very familiar to British shoppers. They are light in colour, clean tasting and sterilized for efficient storage and transport. They are somewhat standard in style and usually come in two strengths, around 3% and around 5%. There are small differences between them and consumer preferences in these beers are usually the result of marketing campaigns.

UK AND IRELAND

Traditional British and Irish beers are ales, the most common of which are Bitter and Stout. Bitter refers to an ale which has a high degree of bitterness, which comes from the addition of a lot of hops. Stout is a dark beer made with roasted malt which gives it a distinctive roasted flavour and colour. France and Belgium are not the best places to buy Bitter or Stout, but in shops geared to British shoppers in and around Calais, you will see cans of familiar names such as John Smith, Tetley, Whitbread Best, Guinness and Murphys. You are unlikely to see brands or types of ale with less mass-appeal.

BELGIUM

For such a small country, Belgium has an amazing number of breweries and types of beer. It is quite hard to categorize Belgian beer, because there are so many different varieties, but they are generally top fermented and bottle matured. Bottle-matured beers are still 'alive' when they go into the bottle, that is they haven't been filtered or pasteurized and so will have some yeasts left in them and will continue to ferment. Some of the types of beer brewed in Belgium are:

White Beers are made with a large proportion of wheat (as opposed to the more usual barley). They produce quite a lot of sediment which makes the beer cloudy, and have an unusual combination of sour and fruity flavours. **Hoegaarden** is a white beer which is familiar now in the UK. **Brugs Tarwebier** is another one to look out for.

Lambics are white beers which ferment spontaneously with wild yeasts similar to those which make cider. The resultant beer has a very distinctive sourness to it, and is also often made in a fruity style. Two quite common types of Lambic are **Gueuze**, which is a blend of old and new Lambics producing a fizzy, slightly sweet beer, and **Kriek** which is flavoured with cherry unlike most beers which are just flavoured with hops. Kriek has a very interesting sour cherry flavour.

Trappist beers may only be produced in one of five monastery breweries in Belgium. They come in three strengths: **Single**, **Dobbel** and **Triple** which range from 6% to 12%. They are all top-quality full-flavoured, dark, fruity, mouth-filling beers, definitely worth investigating. The five breweries are: **Chimay**, **Orval**, **Rochefort**, **Westmalle** and **Westvleteren**. Other beers made in a similar style but not entitled to call themselves Trappist beers are often called **Abbaye/Abbey/Abdij** beers.

Some other Belgian beers to look out for are:
the pale hoppy **La Chouffe**; **Hoegaarden Grand Cru** which is a strong, rich-flavoured aromatic beer; **Gouden Carolus** which is dark and strong; the soft mouth-filling **La Bière des Collines**; and **De Koninck**, which is full flavoured and fruity.

FRANCE

France does not have a particularly good reputation for producing great beer, and indeed quite a lot of it is ordinary-style lager. Much is brewed locally at St. Omer and not far away in Alsace. Although not by any means speciality beers, these compare well with international brands and are often much cheaper. Names to look out for are **La Strasbourgeoise**, **Peterbrau**, **St. Omer**, **La Semeuse**, **Fischer** and **Pelforth**. Although much of the beer produced is lager, many are dark (**Bière Brune**), and have a lot more character than the more familiar light version (**Bière Blonde**).

In addition to the lagers, a lot of excellent, strong top fermented beers are brewed in French Flanders. These are normally referred to as **Bière de Garde**, and usually come in large 75cl bottles. Some excellent ones to look out for are: **CH'TI**, which is dark, rich and malty; **Jenlain**, which has a fruitiness reminiscent of an English Bitter; and **3 Monts**, a fabulous mouth-filling beer with delicate flavour.

GERMANY

Although Germany produces a huge number and variety of beers, the ones you are likely to see in French and Belgian shops are the Pilsener style which originated in the Czech Republic. These beers are dry, golden-coloured, bottom-fermented beers, with distinct hoppiness and floral characteristics. The name is much abused, and should only refer to top-quality beers. Pilseners you are likely to encounter are **Pilsener Urquell** (which is Czech), **Herforder**, **König**, **Dab**, **Holsten** and **Becks**.

Other beer styles that are occasionally seen outside Germany are **Bock**, a strong, dark brown beer, **Münchener** which is a dark brown malty beer at around 5% abv, and **Dortmunder**, a good-quality dry light style of beer.

CIDER AND PERRY

Cider (cidre in French) and Perry (poiré) - which is made from pears - are the two specialities of Normandy, which is outside the area covered in this book. Unfortunately French tastes vary significantly from region to region, and cider is not drunk in any great quantity in the area within easy reach of the Channel Tunnel. Beer is much more the preferred drink here. There is little 'farmhouse cider' available, which is the excellent, distinctive unpasteurized local style produced in small quantities by small producers. Most supermarkets will have a selection of pasteurized ciders of a similar style to those found in Britain. These have less character than unpasteurized ciders. Both standard still and sparkling **doux** (sweet) as well as **Brut** (dry) cider are available along with a few more exciting varieties. Look out for vintage ciders. These have a year printed on the label. They are more interesting drinks due to the extra character of the fruit which comes from a single harvest.

Duty on cider is the same as on beer, so the possible savings are equivalent. Thus 75cl bottles of reasonable quality strong cider cost around 10 F, so they are well worth buying in France if you have a taste for cider.

There is one producer listed in the section on shops where very good unpasteurized cider is made. This is La Maison du Perlé in Loison-sur-Créquoise (see Chapter 16).

CHAPTER 14

Fortified Wines and Spirits

The recent guidelines for the amount of drink which may be brought into the UK from EC countries are 10 litres for spirits and 20 litres for fortified wines. Savings in these categories are probably less than for wine and beer, but they are none the less well worth bringing back. Generally speaking though, the savings are more significant on product brands that are not widely available in the UK.

If you are not buying spirits or fortified wines in France or Belgium it is still worth getting the duty free allowance where good savings can always be made. The allowance is 1 litre for spirits and 2 litres for fortified wines.

Labelling
As with all alcoholic drinks, check the alcoholic strength of anything you buy. This is not just for unfamiliar items. Many standard spirits will come in different strengths, particularly in duty free shops where they are normally 43% as opposed to the usual 40% or 37%. There are few quality classifications of fortified wines or spirits although most names are restricted to drinks made in a specific way and produced in a designated area.

FORTIFIED WINES
Fortified wines are made from a wine base with the addition of

grape spirit. They have an alcohol level of between 15% and 22%. Although Belgium has lower duty than France on fortified wines, prices do not seem to be cheaper across the board.

Port, Sherry and Madeira

The quality and choice of these will generally not be as good as in the UK because they are not traditionally drunk in France in large quantities. At the bottom end of the market savings may be made, as the French tend to use all these fortified wines a great deal in cooking. Belgian supermarkets are probably the best bet if you are intent on buying them.

Vermouth

Vermouth and other aromatized wines are made from a wine base, unfermented grape juice, grape spirit and flavoured alcohol. Vermouth is flavoured with bitter substances. They are not hugely popular in Britain where you see mainly Italian varieties such as Martini and Cinzano readily available. In France there are large numbers of aromatized wines; names include Ambassadeur, Amer Picon, Byrrh, Cazpara, Clarac, Dubonnet, Noilly-Prat and Suze. All these are readily available along with familiar Italian Vermouth such as Campari, Cinzano and Martini at a small discount on UK prices. Each aromatized wine has a very different character, and taste will be very subjective. Worth particular recommendation, however, is Chambery from Savoie.

Vins Doux Naturels

These are wines, often made with Muscat grapes, that are lightly fortified with brandy to produce strong, sweet dessert or aperitif wines. Included in this category are Muscat de Beaumes de Venise, Muscat de Frontignan, Muscat de Rivesaltes, Banyuls, Rivesaltes and Rasteau. These tend to be the best value fortified wines, and are much cheaper than in Britain. They are described fully in the section on wines.

SPIRITS AND LIQUEURS

Familiar Products

Whisky, gin, vodka and liqueurs are generally cheaper than in the UK. The actual savings vary and are not entirely predictable; on some items they are quite large and on others they are insignificant. On a rough comparison between an English supermarket and a French hypermarket I found Grand Marnier was about £5 cheaper, Gordon's Gin was around £3 cheaper, Baileys £2, Smirnoff £2, Glenlivet £2.50, Absolut Vodka £1 and J&B Whisky about £3.50 cheaper. On single-malt whiskys, which normally sell for around £20 in Britain, there was little difference; many were more expensive in France. Anything more expensive than this is almost certainly going to be a better buy in Britain. In general it is better to look for spirits or liqueurs that are less common in Britain to make the biggest savings. For example, **William Lawsons** whisky which is a good blend, but much less common than in France, was good value at 72 F (£9). And if you like aniseed-flavour spirits, don't go for Pernod which is hardly any cheaper, but buy versions such as **Duval** or **51.**

Brandy

Cognac and Armagnac are the two most famous French brandies, and although they use similar grape types their method of production is quite different. At its best, Cognac has more elegance and delicacy than Armagnac, but cheaper Armagnac probably represents the better buy. Traditionally Cognac has been the more popular in Britain and as a result prices for Cognac are much more competitive in the UK. On the basic VS there are only small savings to be made, particularly with the famous names such as **Martell** and **Courvoisier**. The more expensive Cognacs are probably not much cheaper in France. Basic quality Armagnac, however, is much cheaper. I saw **Pallas VS** for about £8 and **Janneau VS** for around £10. Both these prices represent around £5 savings on what you would pay in Britain. Supermarkets also stock many less well-known names, and savings for these can be even bigger.

The other advantage of buying Cognac and Armagnac in France is the enormous choice compared to the UK. Specialist shops often have fantastic selections of rare old Cognacs and Armagnacs which you are unlikely to find elsewhere. These are not going to be terribly cheap though.

When buying Armagnac, look out for **Bas Armagnac** which produces the best quality. **Tenareze** produces light early maturing Armagnac, and **Haut Armagnac** produces the lowest quality. The best Cognac comes from **Grande Champagne**. **Petite Champagne** also produces very fine Cognacs which mature a little earlier. **Fine Champagne** is a mix of the two with at least 50% Grand Champagne. Lesser Cognac, which is used more in blends, comes from **Borderies**, **Fins Bois** and **Bons Bois**. Also important is the age of the brandy. With French brandy and Calvados, however, it is signified by certain terms on the label. In ascending order of age and hence quality: **VS (or 3*)**, **VSOP** and **XO**.

Other brandies produced outside the areas of Cognac and Armagnac are also worth looking out for. They can be excellent quality and very good value. They tend to use the same terms to indicate age.

Other Specialities
There are many interesting spirits and liqueurs available in France which you rarely see in Britain. These will generally be cheaper across the Channel, but are not the sort of things you are going to fill up on. They are interesting, make good gifts, and it is worth buying the odd bottle if you fancy a novelty.

The local speciality in both Belgium and France is **Genever** or **Genièvre** which is a sort of gin. There are many different local variations and specialities, but it tends to be sweeter than English gin. **Genièvre de Houlle** is one example, which is produced near to St. Omer. **Calvados** is the spirit made from distilling cider. It can vary from being delightful to fairly rough and nasty. The choice is infinitely better in France than the UK, and the prices are also much cheaper. Similar terms are used to represent the age as for Cognac and Armagnac. The best Calvados is **Calvados du Pays D'Auge**.

Marc is a spirit made from a distillate of the residue left after grapes are pressed to make wine. Although it doesn't sound very appetizing it can be extremely good. Most regions produce it, with some of the best ones coming from Alsace, Burgundy and Champagne.

Eaux-de-Vie are made by distilling a mash of a given fruit. There are many different types, including fraise (strawberry), framboise (raspberry), prune (plum), coing (quince) and poire (pear) and many more besides. If you are interested in buying some you will need to get a dictionary to work out the various fruits. Served chilled, Eaux-de-Vie are strong in alcohol, dry and colourless. They may come from various parts of France.

Liqueurs are made by flavouring and sweetening a spirit base. Some of the best examples are **Crème** liqueurs which can be drunk on their own or mixed with white wine to make delicious cocktails. The best known is **Crème de Cassis** (blackcurrant) which combines with white wine to make Kir. Many other fruits are used to make crème liqueurs which are just as good, such as **Crème de Framboise** (raspberry) and **Crème de Fraise** (strawberry). The best crème liqueurs come from Alsace, with other good ones made in Burgundy.

Pineau des Charentes is an easily found liqueur made in the Charentais region of France. It is a blend of Cognac and grape juice which is then matured in oak casks. It can be excellent value and is definitely worth seeking out.

PART 2
THE SHOPS

This part of the book deals with the shops where drink can be bought. It is divided into three sections, each of which describes a different route starting from the French side of the Tunnel.

HOW TO READ AN ENTRY

Entries for each shop are set out as follows:

TYPE OF OUTLET   AREA   PAYMENT METHOD

Shop hours

SHOP NAME
Products sold
Brief description

Address

Directions
Tel. no.

What parking is available
Is English spoken?
Tasting?

Further information about shop

Type of Outlet

The entries under 'type of outlet' are: shops, warehouses, drive-in stores, supermarkets and hypermarkets.

Shops in this context means outlets which specialize in drink and give a personal service. The main advantage of shops is that there is usually someone available with knowledge of what is on sale, if you need help.

Warehouses are something of a Calais speciality, set up specifically to cater for cross-channel bulk-buying. They tend to be fairly impersonal places where you wheel a trolley around. Usually there is less opportunity for personal attention than in shops, but sometimes you can get help in warehouses.

Drive-in stores are more aimed at local customers. They are like shops, but you can drive in and load up if you have bought large quantities of drink. Although the choice at these places tends to be quite small, wines may often be tasted, and the level of service can be very good.

Supermarkets are equivalent to British supermarkets, like Tesco's, Sainsbury's, Waitrose, etc. The listings in this category are mainly in Belgium. In northern France there are many, many supermarkets; the names that you might run into are: Shopi, Super U, Pris Unic, Rallaye, Match, Intermarché, Cedico and Uniprix. The selection can be fair, but you will invariably find a larger and better hypermarket or shop nearby. There are some exceptions, which are listed. In Belgium, however, where hypermarkets do not really exist, supermarkets are good places to buy drink. These are described in Chapter 17.

Hypermarkets are a French phenomenon. They are massive supermarkets where you can buy almost anything: cars, washing machines, clothes and more, all on one floor. They are on main roads on the outskirts of towns and have large car-parks. The range of drinks stocked is very large, and the prices are competitive. Buying beer and spirits with familiar brand names is straightforward enough, however buying wine can be a lot more complicated because there is usually very little information about what's inside most of the bottles. Help may be difficult to find but it is always worth asking for the **Conseiller de Vin** (wine adviser), who will give advice. Many will speak some English. If they feel you are serious about buying a significant quantity of wine they may even let you taste something, so it is worth asking. When in supermarkets and hypermarkets always look out for promotions as these often offer amazing value for money. Hypermarkets can get very busy, so it is worth timing your trip. French people tend to have a long lunch-break (as they go home to eat) and so this is often quite a good time to visit. It does mean that there is less chance of getting help though.

* **Area** gives the town or area that the shop is in.

* **Payment method** - Assume that you can pay in French Francs in all outlets in France; and in Belgian Francs in all outlets in Belgium. Otherwise: **£**, **EC** = Eurocard, **A** = Access, **V** = Visa, **Amex** = American Express, **TC** = Travellers cheques, **EChq** = Eurocheques.

* **Products sold** refers to whether wines, beers, spirits or a combination are sold in the specific outlet.

* **Brief description** gives a one-line impression of the shop.

* **Directions** lists directions as to location of the shop.

* **Tasting** gives an indication of whether wines (or other products) may be tasted. Attitudes vary quite a lot and, while tasting is encouraged at some shops, it is strongly discouraged at others. Generally most shops (including hypermarkets) will allow you to taste if you are serious about buying a reasonable quantity. A tasting facility is there as a service to help you choose a bottle of wine, and it is unreasonable to expect it to be a freebie. It is worth negotiating with shop owners; most would be amenable to suggestions such as not charging for a bottle tasted if you subsequently buy a case.

CHAPTER 15

Route 1

Route 1 takes in Calais and follows the direction of the N43 and the A26 autoroute to the south-east.

Calais was never the most beautiful or interesting town in France, and being the centre of the cross-Channel drinks trade has certainly not helped its cause. It has the feel of a frontier-town, and indeed some drink stores are open all night - you get the impression that shady deals are going on in hidden-away warehouses down dark alleys. There is plenty of evidence of vehicles with rear axles buckling under the weight of excess alcohol. However, there are also cafés and restaurants which retain a French atmosphere, the shopping is generally good, and there are plenty of reasonably priced places to stay. But the best reason to stop off in Calais is the unprecedented and astonishing array of places to buy wine, beer and spirits.

The tourist office is in the centre of town between the railway station and the place d'Armes (the main square), at **12 boulevard Clemenceau, Tel. 21 96 62 40**.

A good, reasonably-priced place to stay is the **Hotel Windsor, 2 rue du Commandant Bonningue, Tel. 21 34 59 40** where you can get a very comfortable double room for 230 F. It is well located near the place d'Armes and not far from the ferry terminal. Otherwise, if you fancy something grander with old-fashioned character and charm, try the **Meurice** on **5 rue E. Roche, Tel. 21 34 69 69** which is slightly away from the main hub of Calais. Rooms here start at 325F. Somewhere between these two in terms of grandness is the **Georges V**, also very central on **36 rue Royale, Tel. 21 97 68 00**. This is a fairly characterless hotel, but with good facilities and reasonably priced rooms starting at 300 F. Generally you should not have much difficulty finding a good place to stay in Calais.

There are plenty of places to eat around the place d'Armes and the rue Royale, where you can find a reasonable menu for under 70 F. If you fancy a blow-out, however, head for **Le Channel, 3 bvd de la Résistance Tel. 21 34 42 30**, a gastronomical delight, with menus from 85 F.

If you don't wish to stay in Calais (and who could blame you?) but still want to do your shopping there, you could do a lot worse than **Ardres** which is a pleasant little town just 17km from Calais. The smartest hotel in town is the **Grand Hôtel Clement, 91 esplanade du Marechal Leclerc, Tel. 21 82 25 25**. A cheaper alternative is **Le Relais, bvd C. Senlecq, Tel.. 21 35 42 00**. If you do stay overnight, be sure to visit the shop Le Chai Ardresien listed in this section.

Another place within easy striking distance of Calais is **Recques-sur-Hem** with its fabulous **Chateau de Cocove** which is described in the section on shops. The rooms start at 355 F for a double, and the menus are from 115 F to 335 F.

The first big town off the motorway from Calais is **St-Omer** (46km from Calais) in the heart of the Marais Audomarois, drained marshland which is now a network of canals. St-Omer itself has a small attractive centre with winding cobbled streets, smart boutiques and a lively, bustly feel. The town seems to be full of students, which gives it vibrancy, and on Saturday morning there is an excellent market centred on the place Foch. There are some interesting sites, including an imposing Gothic cathedral and the Chapelle des Jésuits. In the summer you can do a tour of the local waterways by boat. There is full information about the attractions from the **Tourist Information** on **boulevard Pierre Guillain, Tel.. 21 98 08 51**.

A good place to stay in St-Omer is the **Hôtel St. Louis, 25 rue Arras, Tel. 21 38 35 21**, with double rooms from just under 300 F. It is cheap and very comfortable with a lively bar and a very good inexpensive restaurant; an excellent three-course menu is 66 F. A smarter place in town to stay is **Le Bretagne, 2 place du Vainquai, Tel. 21 38 25 78**, or 3 miles north of town in the fabulous but pricey **Château Tilques, rue du Château, Tel. 21 93 28 99**, which is an elegant 52-bedroom château-style hôtel. **Le Cygne, 8 rue Caventou, Tel. 91 28 20 52** is a smart but cosy little restaurant in the town centre with menus starting at around 90 F.

Heading off, up the N43 for a few miles, you will come to Aire-sur-la-Lys (58km from Calais), a pretty little town standing on the confluence of the Lys and two smaller rivers. The focal point of the town is a large cobbled Grande Place in typical Flemish style, bordered by shops and cafés. The most stylish place to stay in

Aire is **Hostellerie des Trois Mousquetaires, Chateau de la Redoute, Tel. 21 39 01 11**. This is a 19th-century château in large grounds with elaborate decor and impeccable service. There is also a good restaurant here. A double room will be around 400 F. A cheaper alternative is the **Europ Hôtel, 14 Grande Place, Tel. 21 39 04 32**, with double rooms from 250 F.

Béthune is not the most beautiful town in the area, but well located just off the A26, and only a 45 minute drive from Calais. The shopping is good in the lively, pleasant centre, and there is a Grande Place with a striking ancient belfry. It makes a convenient stopping place within easy reach of Calais. **Hôtel le Vieux Beffroi, Grande Place, Tel. 21 68 15 00** is very well located right in the centre of town. Although the hôtel is somewhat impersonal, rooms are comfortable and start at around 300 F (double). There is a brasserie and a dining-room in the Hôtel. The menu at 68 F in the brasserie is very good value. Round the corner, on the place de la République, is a good seafood restaurant called **La Taverne**.

SMALL SHOP   CALAIS   A V TC EC AMEX £

09.00-20.00, Thursday to Tuesday

BAR À VINS
Mostly wines and a few spirits
A gem in the centre of Calais

---

52 place d'Armes
62100 Calais

Central Calais
Tel.: 21 96 96 31

Easy parking on street
English spoken
Tasting possible but not encouraged

This is a shop that very much reflects the character of the owner M. Gille, a man who takes his wine very seriously indeed. He is a great character, as charming and French as the wine he sells, but he will not suffer people wasting his time looking for free tasting. The shop is small and the range not large but each wine has been chosen with great care and love. M. Gille has huge authority and makes you feel you are in very safe hands. In choosing the wines, he has looked for exclusivity, and you are unlikely to find his wine elsewhere. The selection is particularly strong in the 20 - 64 F range. There was an attractive white Gascogne at 20 F from Domaine de Tarrit and unusually a red version at the same price; a top-quality Petit Chablis from Daniel Gounot 92 for 64 F and a Côteaux d'Aix en Provence-St. Julien les Vignes 92 for 30 F. The antithesis to the Calais cash-and-carry type stores, this is a place where you follow the chef's recommendation, buy a few bottles, and really impress your friends when you get home.

LARGE WAREHOUSE   CALAIS   A V TC EC £

08.30-20.00, 7 days a week

BEERS ARE US
Mainly beer but good wine and some spirits
Laid-back warehouse geared for English shoppers

RN43
route de St-Omer
62100 Calais

On the N43 towards St-Omer
Tel.: 21 96 95 95

Car-park
English run
Always a few wines on tasting

In this warehouse/shop, they pride themselves on having your favourite beers; Fosters, Stella, John Smiths and Heineken. If you'd ever wanted to see Castlemaine xxxx stacked to the ceiling here's your chance. There is also a selection of local lagers and Belgian beers. The wines on sale are mainly targeted at the lower priced end of the British market: Liebfraumilch, Mateus Rosé and Lambrusco can all be bought at a considerable saving. There is also some better quality, however, with reliable cheapies from Fortant de France at around 20 F and reds from Bulgaria at around 16 F. There is a large section of Burgundy from the reliable producer André Morey at reasonable prices. The big advantage here is that it is a relaxed, pleasant environment, and you avoid the crush of central Calais.

LARGE WAREHOUSE   CALAIS   £ A V ECHQ EC TC

07.00-22.00, every day

CALAIS WINE AND BEER
Wines, beers and some spirits
A superior version of the English style warehouse

---

18 rue de Judée
Z.A. Marcel Doret
62100 Calais
Tel.: 21 97 63 00

Car park
English spoken
Tasting possible with purchases, but not encouraged

This was my favourite of the English-run warehouse shops. It has a good range of wines mostly at the lower end of the price scale but avoids the dingy atmosphere of many of the warehouses. Calais Wine and Beer has probably the best selection in town of non-French wines, including a lot of Italian wines, a selection of Cooks New Zealand wines, several Riojas and Spanish wines from Torres, Australian wines from Penfolds, and Chilean, South African, German and Californian wines. These non-French wines are not the greatest bargains to be had but are generally extremely reliable and at least £1 per bottle cheaper than in the UK. There are still bigger savings to be made on the sparkling wines. The Great Western (Aus) and Freixenet (Sp) were both £2 cheaper than British prices. Aside from these there is a solid selection of French wines with all the major regions represented. The wines are from producers with reputations for making reasonably priced, reliable wines such as Turckheim from Alsace and Rodet from Burgundy. There is a large choice of British favourites like Liebfraumilch and Lambrusco and wines for under a £1 from eastern Europe, Spain and Italy. Calais Wine and Beer stock one type of whisky, gin, vodka and other standard spirits and a good range of competitively priced familiar beers.

SMALL WAREHOUSE   CALAIS   A V AMEX £ EC TC

09.00-19.00, closed Friday and Sunday

CASH AND CARRY B&B
Wines, beers and spirits
Friendly shop which will satisfy most drink needs

24 rue Madrid
62100 Calais

Between place d'Armes and place de Suède
Tel.: 21 34 41 78

Car-parking possible on the street
Reasonable English
Most wines may be tasted

Bernard Cornille, the owner, is a self-confessed wine lover. He is helpful and friendly and will enjoy steering you through his varied collection. When he cannot explain something he'll show you the pages where they're described in an English wine book. The wines range from low-cost English favourites to good, well-priced fine wines. There are plenty of cheaper wines to choose from, including Gascogne whites and reds from the smaller Bordeaux ACs. He had one or two genuine bargains such as a shipment of 4,000 bottles of Châteauneuf-du-Pape intended for Germany sold in the wrong shape bottles at 40 F. The graffiti-covered walls give the place an unpretentious feel and you're bound to end up tasting something. There is a reasonable collection of Belgian beers along with the usual cases of familiar brand lagers. B&B sells a few well-chosen fortified wines and spirits including a cognac VS at 89 F and cheap Pinot de Charentes.

SMALL SHOP   CALAIS   A V EC

9.30-12.15 and 15.00-19.15, Tuesday to Saturday

LES CAVES ST-JEAN
Wine and a few spirits
Small and fairly limited

4 place Crèvecoeur
62100 Calais

Just off boulevard La Fayette
Tel.: 21 36 09 50

Easy parking in nearby place Crèvecoeur
No English spoken
No tasting possible

Not overly friendly small shop with a limited not-too-exciting range of wines. There are some small-producer red Bordeaux at around 30-40 F and a selection of Burgundies from the reliable Bouchard. You might pick up something here to have with a picnic in the square but this shop is not really worth making a detour for.

MEDIUM-SIZED WAREHOUSE   CALAIS
A V EC £ ECHQ

09.30 - 12.00 and 14.00 - 19.00, every day

LE CHAIS
Mainly wine, plus some beer and spirits
A good French-run shop with a large selection of wine

40 rue de Phalsbourg
Centre Frader
62100 Calais

Tel.: 21 97 88 56

Private car-park
English spoken
Extensive tasting possible

Le Chais is a fairly large chain of smart wine shops with two branches in Calais, others in Boulogne and Le Touquet, and one planned for the Cité d'Europe near the Eurotunnel terminal. They claim to be the oldest and biggest wine merchants in the region and are local agents for big wine producers like Louis Jadot, Jaboulet and Lanson. The shop in the rue de Phalsbourg is well laid out, the staff are helpful and many of the wines may be tasted. The wines, which are nearly all French, are mostly in the middle to upper price range and come from good producers. In the price category where the highest savings can be made, there is a good choice of wines from the Loire; Muscadets for under 20 F, Pouilly-Fumé and Sancerre for under 40 F, St Nicolas, Saumur-Champigny and Bourgueil for around 30 F. Additionally, there are a lot of Alsace wines at around 25 F, and a very good selection of Bordeaux reds for under 40 F. There are plenty of wines from Beaujolais and the Côtes du Rhône which are also good value, and several good-value champagnes, with the cheapest at 59 F 80. Le Chais has a fairly small but competitively priced selection of beers, a good choice of spirits including white Eau de Vie, Plum spirit, some reasonably priced Calvados and four different Genièvres. There is a smaller branch of Le Chais on 67 bvd

Jacquard in the centre of town which has a select range of the more expensive wine.

SMALL WAREHOUSE   CALAIS   A V £

08.00 - 20.00, Monday to Friday; and 09.00 to 19.00, Sunday; closed Saturday

CHAMPAGNE CHARLIES
Wine and beers plus a few spirits
A typical Calais warehouse run by the English for the English

14 rue Cronstadt
62100 Calais

Central Calais
Tel.: 21 97 96 49

On-street parking plus drive-in facility
English spoken
Limited tasting possible

This place is a fairly dingy warehouse, geared to bulk purchases of low-cost wines and beers. There is a good range of familiar British brands of beer including Carling Black Label at £10 for 24 cans, McEwans at £10.50, and Stones Bitter for £12.50. There is a drive-in facility and they will help you load straight into your vehicle. The wine selection is uninspiring, with low-cost familiar items such as Liebfraumilch at £2.00 and 1.5 litres of Lambrusco at £1.90 a bottle. There are a number of 3-pack Vins de Table at cheap prices but you would need to taste these before buying. Otherwise, there is a small selection of most of the main French wine regions. An excellent Domaine de Barroque VDP Gascogne at 13 F 95, reasonably priced Chablis ler Cru, a few other Burgundies from lesser-known producers, Loires, Bordeaux, and a few Vins de Pays. One or two spirits are on offer including a Scottish REEL whisky at a mere 58 F a bottle. Rather confusingly, some prices are in Francs and others are in Sterling. There is limited tasting available but this is not really the sort of place to while away time talking about nutty complexity and smoky overtones.

Hypermarket   Calais   A V EC ECHQ £

08.30 - 21.00, Monday to Saturday

CONTINENT
Large range of wines, beers and spirits
A typical large Calais hypermarket

Centre Commercial
avenue Georges Guynemer
62100 Calais

Tel.: 21 97 99 75

Large car-park
English spoken
No tasting

Continent matches up with the biggest Calais hypermarkets. As with Mammouth there is a huge warehouse adjacent to the main part of the shop, piled high with 24 packs of beer. The best value looked like the Continent own label (4.7%) at 33 F for 24 in 25cl bottles. They have a lot of promotions, many of which are cleverly geared towards British customers with things such as Malibu at 59 F and Baileys at 70 F. The best price I saw was 99 F for Pol Roger Champagne, a full £7 cheaper than the usual UK price. Also worth checking out as far as wine is concerned were the 'Les Maîtres Goustiers' label wines. The ones I tried were all good quality and very reasonably priced.

MEDIUM-SIZED WAREHOUSE   CALAIS   A V
   TC
   ECH £

08.00 - 20.00, every day

EASTENDERS
Wines, beers and a few spirits
A place specializing in bulk sales of familiar products

rue Mollien
62100 Calais

Tel.: 21 34 53 33

Car park
English spoken
No tasting

Eastenders have acquired a reputation for being THE bargain-basement Calais warehouse shop, and although they claim to have the best prices in town they are certainly competitive but no cheaper than the hypermarkets or other similar Calais warehouses. They have a good central Calais location and turn-over is brisk. They stock the usual range of familiar canned lagers; Fosters, Castlemaine, Holsten, Stella, etc. as well as a few dirt-cheap French beers. There is a reasonable selection of wine which mainly focuses on cheap names familiar to English shoppers: Lambrusco (18 F a litre), Liebfraumilch (10 F for 75cl), Piat d'Or (18 F) and a couple of Bulgarian whites for under 10 F. Although the place has a distinctly down-market feel, there is also a selection of good wines, some Vacqueyras and Crozes-Hermitage from Jaboulet, a few Beaujolais Cru for under 40 F, some good VDP de Gascogne for 11 F and a reasonable selection of sparkling wines and champagne. Unfortunately you cannot taste wines here and in any case the place does not have an atmosphere conducive to lingering discussions. The staff are friendly but not knowledgeable about wine.

There is a second branch of Eastenders at rue des Garennes where they do discounts if you buy wine or beer by the palate (about 100 cases). As about ten cases is the guideline maximum per person, you need to come armed with an explanation for the customs. The place itself has the look and feel of something out of Mad Max, situated as it is in a very desolate industrial wasteland. Eastenders also have a tobacco shop accross the Belgian border in Veurne. They run a minibus to it from next to the shop in the centre of town.

SMALL WAREHOUSE   CALAIS   A V AMEX £ EC
                                                 TC

08.30-12.30 and 14.00-19.30, closed on Sunday

GRAND CRU MAGNUM
Wines, beers and some spirits
Solid selection, fairly upmarket

---

24 rue Commandant Bonningues
62100 Calais

Between place d'Armes and place de Suède
Tel.: 21 34 58 71

Space available on street for parking
Some English spoken
Tasting on selected wines

This is a small, business-like converted warehouse shop with a solid selection of wines. It mainly caters for locals and tourists who appreciate good-quality wines and don't mind paying the price, although there is also quite a good choice of inexpensive wine. There is a reasonable choice of Bordeaux reds in the 20-40 F range, and quite a good selection of dry white wines for around 20 F from Bergerac, Muscadet and other parts of the Loire. Most other French regions are fairly well represented with good wines from very reliable producers. For example, there are Rhônes from Guigal, Chapoutier and Jaboulet. The house champagne is 68 F and all other major name champagnes are available at minimal discount on the UK price. The shop operates a 10% discount on a case of 12 of the same wine. They stock a fair selection of familiar brand beers but the prices are not the cheapest in town.

MEDIUM-SIZED SHOP   CALAIS   A V TC ECHQ £

09.30 - 12.30 and 14.30 - 19.30, Tuesday to Saturday;
closed Sunday p.m. and all day Monday

INTER CAVES
Wines and a few spirits
A friendly French shop with a good range of wines

28 rue Molien
62100 Calais

Central Calais
Tel.: 21 96 63 82

On-street parking
English spoken
Many wines can be tasted

This is a manageable-sized shop with a good selection of French
wines from all the major regions. The prices are reasonable and
the quality of the wines is generally very good. The staff are very
helpful and the owner, the garrulous Monsieur Van Tittelboom,
will enjoy offering you advice in his enthusiastic but not quite
perfect English. The wines are selected from producers with a
good reputation such as Cave Co-operative de Ribeauville in
Alsace but labelled specially for Inter Caves. Most of the French
regions are represented with a selection of wines covering the
range of prices. The speciality of the house is, however,
Reservavins, which are carefully selected bag-in-the-box wines
which range from 8 F a litre for Vins de Table up to 18 F a litre for
an AOC Bordeaux. The boxes come in 10- or 20-litre sizes, and the
wine keeps well for a few months, so this is a cheap way of buying an everyday wine. All the Reservavins may be tasted on site.
There is a small but carefully selected section of fortified wines
and spirits.

LARGE SUPERMARKET CALAIS A V £ EC ECHQ

09.00-09.00, every day

MAMMOUTH
Wines, beers, and spirits
Big busy hypermarket selling everything you can think of

CC Calais Ouest
route de Boulogne (RN1)
62100 Calais

On the RN1 towards Boulogne
Tel.: 21 34 04 44

Large car-park
Many signs in English and English spoken
No tasting except for some promotions

In addition to the usual Mammouth drinks section there is a separate Sainsbury's drink shop attached. The Mammouth part has the usual massive range of beers, wines and spirits that you would expect in a French hypermarket; and look out for the promotions, there are usually bargains to be had. The beers are in their own separate warehouse (attached to the main part of the store), and there were some of the cheapest beers to be found in town, but don't expect to shop alone as this is probably the busiest hypermarket drinks section in France. There is a comprehensive list of wines but quality is variable and it is worth buying individual bottles to taste first before committing yourself to a large quantity. If you're familiar with what you're buying you'll find some of the best prices around. An obvious advantage of this place is that you can do your other shopping at the same time, because there isn't much that you won't be able to find here. The Sainsbury's section has a selection of the stock you get in a UK branch, with everything between 50p and £2 cheaper than back home, but it feels dull compared to the rest of the hypermarket. Make sure you buy your beer in the Mammouth section.

LARE WAREHOUSE SHOP CALAIS A V £ EC ECHQ

08.00 - 20.00, every day

PERADEL
Large range of wines, beers and spirits
A friendly place with a large selection of wine

rue Marcel Doret
ZI Marcel Doret
62100 Calais

Tel.: 26 69 30 30

Car-park
English spoken
Many wines may be tasted

Peradel is a large up-market French-run warehouse shop. Everything there is well presented, and it is a nice place to wander around. The initial impression is of a smart shop and what they have is very competitively priced. There is a fairly small selection of bottled beer, including cheap local brews such as PeterBrau and La Strasssbourgeoise. The Stella Artois was the cheapest I saw anywhere, at 42 F for 24 x 25cl bottles (this works out far cheaper than buying it in 50cl cans). The wine ranged from around 15 F for a Côtes du Frontonnais up to thousands for top Bordeaux from a fair choice of vintages. There is a reasonable choice of red Bordeaux in the under 40 F range. The producers from other regions are mainly well known and top quality. Surprisingly the prices for many of these seemed significantly cheaper than those in the UK. The Chablis all looked good value, including a Moreau 93 for 48 F (probably £2 cheaper than in the UK), St-Véran Domaine des Deux Roches at 46 F and a Beaune 1er Cru 1990 Les Epenottes for 46 F. Otherwise there was plenty to choose from of Loire and Alsace wines and an excellent range of well-priced champagnes, including Pol Roger at 99 F and Joseph Perrier at 93 F. Peradel has a good selection of fortified wines and spirits; look out for their own label Ratafia, a delicious aperitif from the Champagne region. There is a 'degustation' bar where a selection of wines are on tasting, but the very helpful Mme Janot told me that other wines can be opened for customers serious about buying a reasonable quantity.

SUPERMARKET   CALAIS   A V £ E CHEQUES

Open 24 hours a day, 7 days a week

PIDOU CASH AND CARRY
Large range of wines, beers and spirits
A large supermarket open 24 hours a day

21 rue Marcel Dassault
62100 Calais

Tel.: 21 96 51 62

Car-park
Information in English
No tasting

Pidou is a large French-run supermarket with all the usual cheap favourites. There is a good selection of beers all competitively priced, a large range of fortified wines and spirits and a fairly big selection of wine. Buying wine here is very much a matter of pot-luck. There is plenty at the cheaper end of the scale but most of the producer's names are unfamiliar, and the safest thing to do might be to try a bottle out in the car-park. Otherwise it might be best to stick to beer or familiar names. The advantage of this shop is that it is open 24 hours a day, but it is very large and chaotic and you won't find any staff to help you. Apart from drink there is a selection of perfume, food and other last-minute souvenirs. This place will not offer you a memorable shopping experience but might fit the bill when other places in Calais are closed.

SMALL SPECIALIST CHAMPAGNE SHOP
CALAIS   A V EC £

10.00 - 20.00, every day

ROYAL CHAMPAGNE
Produce from the Champagne region
A delightful specialist champagne shop

9 rue Gerschell
62100 Calais

Just off the rue Royale near the Casino
Tel.: 21 96 51 62

On-street parking
No English spoken
No tasting

Annick Ehrlich is the most enthusiastic advocate of champagne you're ever likely to meet. The shop is tiny, only selling about a dozen items, but the amount of explanation about every aspect of champagne that Mme Ehrlich gives is remarkable. She will tell you all about different champagnes: their optimum temperatures, the matches of specific champagnes with food, and the dubious goings-on of the unscrupulous large champagne houses. If you ever want your bottle of champagne explained down to the last bubble, come to this shop. She offers a personally selected range from basic non-vintage at 68 F through Premier Cru to vintage, all very reasonably priced. There are also a few more unusual items such as the still wine Coteaux Champenois and the aperitif Ratafia. After all the explanation, this is a difficult place to escape from empty handed.

SMALL SHOP CALAIS A V £ EC

09.00-12.30 Tuesday to Saturday; and 09.30-13.00, Sunday

LE TERROIR
Over 3,500 different wines and spirits
A small shop packed full of interesting things

29 rue Fontinettes
62100 Calais

Just off boulevard Lafayette
Tel.: 21 36 34 66

Nearby on-street parking
Some English spoken
Tasting possible on cheaper wines for large purchases

Le Terroir is small but packed to the rafters with a huge selection of wines and spirits. This shop has everything from wine en Vrac at 7 F 50 a litre to ancient Grand Cru classes at 15,000 F. You can spend ages marvelling at the wines from all over France but perhaps even more unusual are the selections of spirits, old Armagnacs, Calvados, Eaux de Vie, Cognacs and aperitifs. M. Morvan who runs the place proudly declared that it is the oldest wine shop in Calais, the most individual, and the one where people come to find things they can't find elsewhere. After seeing it, I can believe him. Not everything is rare and expensive though; there is a good range of red Bordeaux for under 40 F, relatively cheap spirits and champagne. There are Rhônes and Burgundies from reliable producers; a Hautes-Côtes de Beaune from Chanson at 33 F 50 was very good value. The nice thing about shops like this one is that you can come in to look at all the wonderful rarities but still find inviting bottles at under 20 F.

MEDIUM-SIZED SHOP TUNNEL TERMINAL
A V EC AMEX TC £

Open 24 hours

EUROTUNNEL DUTY FREE
Wine, beer and spirits
A good place to pick up duty free spirits

Terminal Tourisme
62231 Coquelles

At the Eurotunnel terminal
Tel.: 21 00 42 82

Large car-park
English spoken
No tasting

This 400 m^2 shop is definitely worth visiting, picking up your litre of duty free spirits here - spirits are cheaper than you will find in duty-paid shops particularly when you consider that they are 43% alcohol by volume - and it offers the best selection of malt whiskies of any Cross-Channel duty free operator.

The wines are well chosen, mostly non-French wines that you will have difficulty finding in France. Whilst the prices are not the cheapest and your duty free allowance is limited to two litres per person, you are entitled to combine this allowance with that of the outward bound trip's visit in the Folkestone Terminal outlet.

There is also likely to be a duty-paid wine shop at the terminal in the near future. A good place to get rid of any unspent French francs.

Large supermarket   Cité d'Europe
£ A V EC ECHQ

10.00 - 20.00, Monday to Thursday; 10.00 - 21.00, Friday; 9.00 -
20.00, Saturday; closed on Sundays
TESCO
Wines, beer and spirits
A huge selection of all imaginable drinks

Centre de Commerce et Loisir
Cité d'Europe
1001 Boulevard de Kent
62231 Coquelle

Cité d'Europe
Tel.: 21 46 47 48
3,500 space car-park
English spoken
Many wines on tasting

Cité d'Europe is an immense regional shopping centre under one
roof, due to be opened on 22 March 1995, next to the Eurotunnel
terminal. It will have a European theme, and is aiming to attract
shoppers from Holland and Belgium as well as the British and
locals. The Tesco's will be huge; 17,600 sq. ft. of selling space (the
size of a very large supermarket) devoted almost entirely to
drink. They are aiming to combine the excitement of a French
hypermarket with the reliability and service of their brand name.
There are due to be over 1,200 lines, including everything from
the most expensive Bordeaux to the cheapest Vin de Table. The
wines will come from over 27 countries of origin, including
unusual places such as Brazil and Mexico. Beer will be sold by the
bottle and by the case, and there will be flat-bed trolleys to enable
easy loading. There will also be a very large selection of all imaginable fortified wines and spirits. Tesco's are aiming to have good
customer service with a good selection of wines open and on tasting, but also the possibility of wines being opened at the customer's request.

There is also to be a Carrefour hypermarket (see section on
Dunkerque) and a Le Chais shop (see this chapter) at Cité
d'Europe.

WAREHOUSE SHOP   NR. TUNNEL TERMINAL
A V EC £ TC

08.30 - 19.30, Monday to Friday; 07.30 - 18.30, Saturday; and 09.00 - 18.00, Sunday

FRANGLAIS
Wines, beers and spirits
A relaxed place to buy from a standard range

CD 215
Fréthun
62185 Calais

On autoroute, head towards Boulogne and follow signs for TGV, then pick up signs for Franglais
Tel.: 21 85 29 39

Large car-park
English spoken
Most wines may be tasted

Although Franglais is located out of the centre of Calais in a fairly desolate site next to the village of Fréthun it is easily accessed from both ferry and Channel Tunnel terminals. The shop is very much geared to the British customer - the staff all speak English and the prices are displayed in both English and French. The wine is mainly French and although most regions producing low to medium-priced wines are covered, there are few exciting surprises or terribly imaginative selections. John Woolnough who runs the shop believes that few people buying wine in Calais will be 'wine buffs' with preset ideas, and so he has organized a tasting room where nearly all of the 300 wines on offer in the shop can be sampled at leisure. There is a reasonable selection of beers although probably not the rock-bottom cheapest in Calais, and there is a standard range of spirits. This is a relaxed easy-going establishment with some cheap wines but don't expect an exciting French shopping experience.

Small Shop   Ardres   A V EC £

10.00 - 19.00, every day
LE CHAI ARDRESIEN
Wines, beers and spirits
A friendly wine shop with plenty of good buys

681 ave. de Calais
62610 Ardres

In Ardres, on the N43
Tel.: 21 36 26 26

Easy on-street parking
English spoken
Several wines on tasting

Paul Jones who runs Le Chai Ardresien with his wife Beatrice clearly loves his new-found occupation of being a wine merchant. He is very enthusiastic about wines, and enjoys introducing new wines to the uninitiated. The shop is small but packed full with a very impressive range of French wines, spirits and liqueurs. The policy of the shop is to choose wines which have received good write-ups in the highly regarded French wine guide books: Hachette and Dussert-Gerber. The wines held in stock are constantly changing, but they are generally from small producers and competitively priced. All French regions are included, with a particularly good selection of wines from the Loire, and plenty of Champagne and Méthode Champenoise. There are also lots of unusual Eaux de Vie from peach, quince and thyme, provencal aperitifs and crème liqueurs from Burgundy and Alsace. There is a reasonable selection of beers including Newcastle Brown and Biddenden Cider. Tasting evenings are organized when a 4 course meal is served, with a different wine for each course and digestifs to follow. The meal costs 100 F, you can drink as much as you want, and the whole evening sounds like a lot of fun. You need a minimum of twelve people to book these evenings. The big attraction of this shop is that, although only 20 minutes from Calais, the place feels like a million miles from it. You are in a proper French village, away from the crowds in a relaxed and friendly atmosphere.

Château Hôtel   Between Calais and St-Omer   £ EC A V Amex

07.00 - 24.00, every day
CHATEAU DE COCOVE
Wines, beers and spirits
A fabulous hotel where you can buy high top quality wine

The Wine Shop
Chateau de Cocove
62890 Recques-sur-Hem

Follow signs off the N43
Tel.: 21 82 68 29

Large car-park
English spoken
Wines can be sampled by the glass in bar and restaurant

Château de Cocove is a beautiful 3-star Château-Hôtel set in its own grounds near the village of Recques-sur-Hem. The Château has a cellar where you can buy from a good range of wines. The atmosphere is serious and the cellars of a 17th-century château must be everybody's fantasy of where wine should be bought. Despite the grandeur of the setting, however, there is a reasonable selection of wines under 40 F. There was a Château Beausoleil 1992 Bordeaux, good value at 25 F, some good Vins de Pays, the excellent Champagne Gardet is 84 F 50, a very good Alsace Gewürztraminer at 35 F and a fine Château Loudenne 1991 for 48 F. There is a fairly rapid turnover of the cheaper wines so few on the list will remain the same, but the current promotions are definitely worth looking into. The majority of the wine, however, is top-quality, fine Burgundy from the producer Chanson, and Cru Classe Reds and Sauternes from Bordeaux. The prices of many of these won't be any cheaper than in Britain but this is a wonderful atmosphere in which to buy a bottle or two. I was shown round by Somellier Xavier Lamarche who was helpful and clearly took his work very seriously. Although grand, the hotel is not outrageously expensive: double rooms start at 355 F and there are amazing-looking menus from 11 5 to 335 F. They also do two gastronomical packages and various weekend specials.

HYPERMARKET   ST-OMER   A V EC ECHQ £

09.00 - 21.00, Monday to Saturday

HYPER CEDICO
Wines, beers and spirits
A large hypermarket

RN43
62500 St-Martin-au-Laert

On the RN43 in St-Martin, just outside St-Omer
Tel.: 21 88 79 00

Large car-park
Information in English
No tasting

From the point of view of ease of finding your way around, this branch of Hyper Cedico is perhaps the best hypermarket in the area. Go to the information desk and you will be given a helpful map of the store. There are several English-speaking staff here who wear Union Jack badges. The wine selection is not immense by hypermarket standards and there are no great surprises, but there is plenty here in each price category. Cedico is part of a large group which has recently been bought up by Tesco, a selection of whose wines is available here. These provide a safe option, reliable wines guaranteed to be £1 cheaper than in the UK. Bigger savings can be made buying non-Tesco wine but, as with all French supermarkets, it is a hit and miss affair. The beer selection is extremely good. There are a lot of local brews from St-Omer as well as several Belgian beers: Chimay red, Chimay blue, Gueuze, Kriek and Orval amongst others. There are also several familiar brands seen in the UK such as Kronenbourg and Stella at competitive prices. The fortified wines and spirits are fairly standard: Pernod is worth buying at 77 F 25 a litre, and there were some bargain Muscats (de Rivesaltes, de Lunel and de Frontignan) starting at 25 F. The big attraction of this place, however, is the relaxed atmosphere away from the Calais crush, the well-displayed stock and the English-speaking staff.

HYPERMARKET ST-OMER A V EC £ ECHQ

09.00 - 21.00, Monday to Saturday (open to 22.00 on Friday)

MAMMOUTH
Large range of wine, beer and spirits
A large hypermarket

Centre Commercial Maillebois
route d'Arques
62500 Longuenesse

On the N42 towards Longuenesse
Tel.: 21 98 78 00

Large car-park
Some information in English
Tasting possible

This is a much bigger hypermarket than the Hyper Cedico which is a mixed blessing. While there is a greater choice, particularly of wines and spirits, it is much harder to sift through. They are also not nearly as tuned in to English customers, so you are much more on your own here. As with all French supermarkets check out the promotions, they can be fantastic bargains. I saw Corbières at 8 F 50 and Minnervois at 9 F 95. But, before you buy anything in quantity, try it first. Tasting is not encouraged but if you can convince the 'Chef du Rayon' that you are going to buy a large quantity he might let you. There is a good range of beers, with many Belgian beers included, plus the usual good value packs of 24. The local St-Omer lager was 29 F 95 for 24 x 25cl bottles. If you like experimenting with liqueurs and aperitifs you could be happy for years - every fruit and herb seems to be represented. If you enjoy Armagnac, check out the prices because there are usually good savings to be made.

Medium-sized shop   St-Omer   A V EC

09.30 - 12.00 and 14.30 - 19.00, Tuesday to Saturday

CAVES DU PRODUCTEUR
Wines and a few spirits
A great place to buy Bordeaux wine

52 rue Frères Camus
62219 Longuenesse

In the small village of Longuenesse
Tel.: 21 62 50 80

Parking is easy in Longuenesse
A little English spoken
Nearly all the wine may be tasted

See the entry for Bruay-la-Buissière (below)

Large shop   St-Omer   A V EC £

09.15 - 12.15 and 14.00 - 19.00, Tuesday to Saturday

CAVES ST. ARNOULD
Wines, beers and spirits
A large French wine shop with a comprehensive range

114 rue de Calais
62500 St-Omer

In central St-Omer off boulevard de Strasbourg
Tel.: 21 38 07 24

Pay-zone parking in town centre, also a drive-in facility
English spoken
Tasting possible

The St. Arnould group is a huge company involved in wholesale and retail of drinks, bottling wine, and brewing. The shop in the centre of St-Omer has a good range of carefully selected French wines which cover all prices, from 7 F 60 for table wine to thousands for the best Bordeaux. The shop is on three floors, with the best wines naturally in the cellar and the lesser wines on the other two floors. There is a tasting room where some wines are open and available for tasting and others may be opened if the customer is serious about buying a reasonable quantity. As usual in this area of France, the best selection of reasonably priced reds, comes from Bordeaux, with a good choice of Bordeaux Supérieur, Côtes de Bourg, Canon-Fronsac and Côtes de Castillon for under 30 F. There are also cheap Cahors, Buzet, Bergerac and Côtes du Rhône. The white wines are more expensive, with only the Loires really in the cheap category. There are several good-value champagnes, the pick of which is the Champagne Gardet, a real bargain at 70 F. Les Caves St. Arnould has a large range of interesting beers including several from Belgium - the local beers Facon, Semeuse and La Bière de St-Omer which are actually brewed by the St. Arnould group, and the standard international brands. Prices for well-known brands of beer are not as competitive as in Calais though. There is also a large selection of spirits although there are no particular bargains there. The staff were helpful and knowledgeable.

SMALL SHOP   NR. ST-OMER   TC ECHQ

09.00-20.00, every day
LE CHAI JOLIBOIS
Wines only
A friendly shop with a small but good selection of wine

---

21 RN42
62380 Setques

Just off the A26 on the RN42
Tel.: 21 39 70 59

Parking possible on the road outside the shop
A little English spoken
Most wines may be tasted

Although this is a tiny shop with a very small selection of wines, it is a really nice place to come to buy and not be overawed by a bewildering range. The wines turn over fairly quickly but are mostly from Bordeaux, the south-west and the Loire. The owner Véronique Holland has selected interesting wines aiming generally around the 15-30 Franc mark. There were some quite unusual wines when I visited; an excellent dry white Cadillac for 20 F and a red Pécharmant at 35 F. The small size of the list means that Veronique is very clued up on everything she sells and offers advice enthusiastically in a mixture of French and English. She reckons that champagne is overpriced and so doesn't stock it, but sells a sparkling Saumur for 50F instead which she rates very highly. You can buy wine en Vrac and Veronique will lend you a 5 litre container to take it away in. Bought like this it must be drunk quickly before it oxidizes unless you are going to bottle it yourself.

SMALL SHOP   NR. ST-OMER   ECHQ

09.15 - 12.15 and 14.15 - 19.15, Tuesday to Saturday

MAISON PECRO
Wines, beers and spirits
A very French, family wine business

12 route de Wisques
62219 Longuenesse

On the road towards Wisques from Longuenesse
Tel.: 21 38 08 64

Easy parking on street
Minimal English
Tasting possible with intended purchase

Longuenesse is the smart quiet suburb of St-Omer which makes it a convenient place to shop and avoid the hassle of the town centre. Maison Pecro is a typical small French wine business, and has been in the family since 1919. Their main business comes from wholesale supply to shops and restaurants but all the wines are available in the shop. Do not be deceived by the small size of the shop as there is 800 m² cellar space at the back. M. Pecro is a Négociant buying wines direct from small producers, and bottling many of the wines on site. Their list is huge, including wines from all the main French regions. Prices range from a few francs for Vins de Table to several hundred for top growths. They have a very fine selection of smaller Bordeaux Châteaux, from around 15 F for Bordeaux Supérieur and a particularly good choice of Pomerol and St-Emilion in the 30-50 F price bracket, which you would certainly not find in the UK. The list of beers is impressive even though very few of them are on display in the shop. There is a reasonable selection of pastis, brandies and other spirits.

MEDIUM-SIZED SHOP   BÉTHUNE   A V EC

09.15 - 12.15 and 14.15 - 19.15; closed on Tuesday morning and Sunday

CAVE DES TREILLES
Wines, beers and spirits
A smart city-centre shop with a good choice of beers

15 place Jules Senis
62400 Bethune

Town centre very near the Grande Place
Tel.: 21 56 96 03

On-street parking, payment required
No English spoken
Only wine sold en Vrac may be tasted

This shop in the centre of Béthune has a carefully chosen selection of classic French wines. They start at 6 F a bottle for the Cuvée du Patron Vin de Table and go up into the hundreds of francs for the top Bordeaux. The major regions are well represented but there are few surprises to set the pulse racing. Although some of the cheaper AOCs from the south are here, the bulk of the wine is Mid to High price. There are, however, three wines sold en Vrac and you could get a 15-litre party barrel of Vin de Table for a mere 60 Francs. There is a good selection of French liqueurs, Cognac and Eaux de Vie from strawberry, blackcurrant and plum, but the highlight of the shop has to be the terrific selection of Belgian beers beautifully presented and just asking to be sampled.

HYPERMARKET BÉTHUNE A V EC

08.30 - 22.00; closed on Sundays (open on Sundays in December)

HYPER AUCHAN
Huge range of wines, beers and spirits
A large busy hypermarket

La Rotonde
62400 Béthune

On the way into town from the A26
Tel.: 20 68 28 28

Car-park
Some English spoken
Tasting for wines on promotion

Each French hypermarket that you come across seems to be bigger than the last. The Auchan in Béthune is an enormous round building with a vast wine, beer and spirits section. Although not exactly geared to British customers, there is a very friendly 'Conseiller des Vins' called Freddy Manbour who will do his best to help you in his broken English. He is easy to recognize because of his handlebar moustache, and is there most mornings and all day on Friday and Saturday. The range of still and sparkling French wines, apéritifs, spirits and liqueurs is enormous. There is a standard selection of beer for sale by the 6, 12 or 24 at good prices. This place can get busy on Saturdays with 'animateurs' with microphones calling out discounts and special offers. There are always promotions which are worth investigating. There was a very attractive-looking 18-bottles of Côtes de Duras red for 167 F when I was there. As with all hypermarkets, however, quality is variable and anything bought in bulk should be tasted first.

MEDIUM-SIZED SHOP   BRUAY-LA-BUISSIÈRE
A V EC

09.30 - 12.00 and 14.30 - 19.00, Tuesday to Saturday

CAVES DU PRODUCTEUR
Wines and a few spirits
A great place to buy Bordeaux wine

52 rue Emile Basly
62700 Bruay-la-Buissière

In Zone 3 of Bruay
Tel.: 21 62 50 80

Parking in street outside shop
No English spoken
Nearly all the wine may be tasted

This is a good place to buy cheap Claret (red Bordeaux), particularly if you suffer from multibottlephobia. The shop is very man-
ageable with a short list to choose from, but a high proportion in
the interesting under-60 F range. There are several wines en Vrac;
AC Bordeaux 93 is 16 F/ltr, Cotes de Bourg 92 is 19 F/ltr, Medoc
92 is 25 F/ltr and Lussac-St-Emilion 92 is 27 F/ltr. You can buy
good-quality 10-litre containers with taps which will keep the
wine for three months; or cheaper plastic containers which will
keep it for one month. The bottled wines are mostly from the
lesser ACs; there is a selection of vintages of Château Baffort - a
Premières Côtes de Blaye - at around 25 F, Cotes de Bourg,
Fronsac, minor St-Emilions, and one of each of the major ACs. All
are reasonably priced. All of the wine en Vrac, and most of the
other bottles, can be tasted. Apart from the red Bordeaux there
are a few white Bordeaux, a couple of Alsace, a rosé from
Bordeaux, a Méthode Champenoise, and a champagne for 91 F.
There is a small but interesting selection of Eaux de Vie and
brandies. Mme Emblanc who runs this shop is very chatty and
friendly but unfortunately doesn't speak any English. Buying
wine in a place like this is good fun - you can taste most of what's

on offer, there are huge potential savings to be made, and it is quite a different experience from anything in the UK.

MEDIUM-SIZED SHOP   LIÉVIN.   A V EC

09.30 - 12.00 and 14.30 - 19.00, Tuesday to Saturday

CAVES DU PRODUCTEUR
Wines and a few spirits
A great place to buy Bordeaux wine

2 rue Jean Baptiste Defernez
62153 Lievin

Tel.: 21 44 32 70

Nearly all the wine in the shop may be tasted

Lievin is further down the A26 near Lens. There is no particular attraction to the town, except that access to the motorway and hence Calais is very good. For details of shop, see entry for Bruay-la-Buissière.

Route 2

This route takes the A16 south from the Tunnel to Boulogne. It heads south down the D940 to Berck-sur-Mer, then inland to the east via Montreuil, Hesdin and St-Pol-sur-Ternoise, and eventually ends up at Arras.

Wissant is on the coast, 20km south of Calais on the D940. The fact that it is half-way between Calais and Boulogne - with easy access to both, a good sandy beach and a pleasant seasidey feel - make it an excellent place to stop off. There are a few hotels to stay in. **Hôtel de la Plage, place Edouard Houssin, Tel. 21 35 91 87** was quite shabby but is in the process of being done up. Double rooms with en suite bathroom cost 275 F. It has a friendly informality, and a family-oriented feel. There is an atmospheric restaurant in the hotel with a choice of good, reasonably priced menus. Next door is the smarter **Normandie, place du Verdun**, Tel. **21 35 90 11** and across the road is the cosy and comfortable **Le Vivier, Tel. 21 35 93 61** with double rooms from 290 F. Le Vivier has an excellent fish restaurant.

Wimereux is another place to stop off a little further down the same sandy coast. It has a similar fading seaside-resort feel to it as Wissant, but is a little bigger and has good shopping; there are two places to buy wine, plus one in nearby Wimille. You are only a few miles outside Boulogne, so it makes a good base from which to visit. The best hotel in Wimereux is the **Atlantic, Digue de Mer, Tel. 21 32 41 01** with double rooms from 350 F. It also has an excellent restaurant and cheaper brasserie. A cheaper alternative is the **Speranza, 43 Générale de Gaulle, Tel. 21 32 46 09**.

Boulogne like Calais is a channel port, a short hop from Dover with regular SeaCat and ferry crossings. It is a large town situated just 34km south-west of Calais but has none of the tackiness of its more famous neighbour. Boulogne is laid back and has retained a good deal of its French fishing port character. Fish are sold on the quayside, there is an attractive old town and there is a commercial rather than an industrial feel to the place which makes it more pleasant for visitors than Calais. It is a good place for shopping, and most French food delicacies are available in plentiful supply in the town centre. There is also a very good selection of places to buy beer, wine and spirits. However, there aren't too many places to stay in the centre. I found the **Hôtel de Lorraine, 7 place de Lorraine, Tel. 21 31 34 78** comfortable if a little characterless. It is very central. Double rooms with wash basin start at 190 F. Good places to eat nearby are **Le Marivaux** in the **place Gustave Charpentier** which does a simple but good 3-course meal for 68 F, or the more expensive but classier **L'Huiterie at 11 place Lorraine**. The best restaurant in town is the Michelin-starred **La Matelote, 80 boulevard Ste Beuve**, which is renowned for its seafood.

Le Touquet is a very smart resort complete with a sea-front promenade and very grand-looking hotels and appartments. It doesn't have the charm of Wissant or Wimereux, but if you are after a 4-star hotel and a night at the casino, this could be the place to come. There is no shortage of hotel space in Le Touquet. There is the reasonably priced **La Regence, 17 rue de la Paix, Tel. 21 05 12 44** or the grander and more comfortable **Ibis Thalassa, Front de Mer, Tel. 21 09 87 00** which overlooks the sea. **Serge Perrard, 67 rue de Metz, Tel. 21 05 13 33** is an excellent sea-food restaurant specializing in fish soup.

Berck-sur-Mer is a more low-key resort with a good sandy beach, a relaxed atmosphere and plenty of accommodation. A good place to stay is **Le Littoral, 36 av. Marianne Toute Seule, Tel. 21 09 07 76** which is comfortable and reasonably priced.

Turning inland along the D917, you arrive at **Montreuil-sur-Mer** which is a pretty little cobbled town built on a hill, and not by the sea as the name suggests. Montreuil is a very pleasant place to wander around, stay for a night or two and eat in great style. The English-run **Le Shakespeare, 7-9 rue de Change, Tel. 21 86 16 04** is a little shabby, but cheap and very friendly, with a cosy bar which feels like a front room. Bed and Breakfast here starts at 140 F per person. If you fancy something smarter, stay in **Les Hauts de Montreuil** (see shop section), where you can get a very comfortable double room for 350 F. This is also an excellent place to eat and buy wine. The really luxurious place to eat and stay in town, however, is **Le Château de Montreuil, 4 chaussée des Capucins, Tel. 21 81 53 04**. Serious food at serious prices, but still a bargain compared to London.

Hesdin is an attractive town without quite the charm of Montreuil. The highlight is the 16th-century town hall and bell tower. A good place to stay here is **La Chope, 48 rue d'Arras, Tel. 21 86 82 73**.

In between Montreuil and Hesdin there is some lovely countryside; turn left at the village of **Beaurainville** and drive up the **Vallée de Créquoise** and on to the village of **Fressin**.

The final place in this section is the city of **Arras**, which has a beautiful centre of stunning Flemish architecture. There is a double town square of the Grande Place and the place des Héros where the town hall stands with its imposing belfry. Arras has plenty of interesting shops and attractive restaurants. **Le Diamant, 5 place des Héros, Tel. 21 71 23 23** is a comfortable place to stay right in the centre. A single room there costs 210 F. The unfortunately named **OK Pub** nearby on the **place de la Vacquerie** really is OK, and does good simple food with a good selection of Belgian beers. **Les 3 Luppars, 49 Grande Place, Tel. 21 07 41 41** is another reasonably priced, centrally located hotel. The place to eat is **La Faisanderie, 45 Grande Place, Tel. 24 48 20 76**. It is situated right on the Grande Place and provides haute cuisine in a beautiful setting.

Small Shop   Wimereux   A V EC TC

07.00-21.00, Friday to Wednesday

LE TERROIR
Wine, beer and spirits
An Aladdin's Cave for wine and spirits enthusiasts

16 rue Carnot
62930 Wimereux

On the main street in Wimereux, opposite Ma Normandie
Tel: 21 32 41 33

Pay-zone parking
Limited English spoken
Some tasting possible

M. and Mme Corteyn are real characters who clearly get a lot of pleasure out of running this amazing little shop. They stock food delicacies and an incredible selection of antique wines. They have wines from every vintage since 1949 and Armagnacs going back even further; they recommend them as birthday presents. Apart from these the cellar is full of strange and wonderful things such as Château Pétrus, Châteaux Yquem and other top Bordeaux from the best vintages. There are wines from most of the other French regions including big-name Burgundies, Rhones, Loires and Alsaces as well as more unusual bottles from the Jura, Savoie and Switzerland. In addition to the Armagnac there are many different spirits: Eaux de Vie made from pear, plum and ginger, and rum from Brasil, Peru and Martinique, as well as a large selection of unusual beers. Even if I could remember everything M. Corteyn showed me, I would not tell you because that would spoil the fun of visiting the shop. Not everything is rare and expensive, however, there are plenty of cheaper wines including some very reasonable Vins de Pays and Bordeaux Supérieur. Definitely worth a visit.

SMALL SHOP   WIMEREUX   A V TC £ EC

08.00-12.30 and 15.00 - 19.30; closed Sunday p.m. and Wednesday out of season

MA NORMANDIE
Mainly wine, a few spirits, some beers
A pleasant little wine and cheese shop

29 rue Carnot
62930 Wimereux

On the main street in Wimereux
Tel: 21 32 45 71

Pay-zone parking near the shop
Some English spoken
Some wines on tasting

Ma Normandie is a small cheese and wine shop also selling fresh eggs, fish soup and various other delicacies. The choice is fairly small, but there are some good-quality classic French wines there. These are mainly from Bordeaux, but with some Burgundy, Loire, Rhône, Champagne and one or two Vins de Pays thrown in. The Bordeaux included some of the ACs which are less well known in the UK such as Canon-Fronsac, Premières Côtes de Blaye and Côtes de Bourg. These are in the 30-60 Franc range. There are more expensive wines from the Haut-Médoc, St-Emilion and Pomerol from well-known producers Moueix. The Burgundies and Rhônes come from reliable producers such as Drouhin, Rodet and Jaboulet. There is a little corner of the shop very invitingly set up for tasting cheese as well as wine and although you won't find the best bargains in the region here this is the sort of very French place which is most enjoyable to visit.

NÉGOCIANT/MERCHANT WIMILLE (NR. BOULOGNE) A V EC EC

08.30-12.00 and 13.30-17.30, Tuesday to Friday; open on Saturday every other week

ETIENNE LEBEURRE
Wines, a few spirits and local speciality beers
A traditional wine merchant well worth visiting

46 rue Générale de Gaule
62126 Wimille

On the main road in Wimille
Tel: 21 32 01 06

Easy parking on street
A little English spoken
Tasting possible for intended purchases

Etienne Lebeurre is a traditional firm which has been going since 1902. They do not have a huge selection of wines, but everything has been carefully chosen, and efficiency and friendliness radiate from the staff who clearly work in a business they love. Some of the cheaper wines are bottled on site and there is a pretty good choice in most categories. In the under-20 F range there are red wines from Provence, Cahors, Pays de L'Aude and several from Bordeaux. There is a good selection of Loire whites and reds, with nearly everything including Pouilly-Fumé and Sancerre under 40 F. The house champagne is 65 F 50, an excellent champagne from a small grower/producer is 84 F and there are plenty of sparkling wines from 12 to 38 F. Most of the other regions of France are represented by good-quality but reasonably priced producers. There are a few specialty Douai-brewed beers including the aptly named Bière du Démon at a diabolical 12% proof. The highlight of the visit was tasting an Eau de Vie de Fleur de Bière, which had an amazing Christmas pudding aroma and was delicious. There are one or two other unusual aperitifs and an intriguing-looking rhubarb cider.

SUPERMARKET   WIMILLE   A V EC ECHQ

09.00-20.00, Monday to Saturday

PG
Good range of wine, beer and spirits
Very civilized superior supermarket

99 rue Raoul Lebeurre
62630 Wimille

Off the D940 just outside Wimereux
Tel: 21 32 45 40

Large car-park
A little English spoken
Tasting possible

See comment for PG in Boulogne

HYPERMARKET   BOULOGNE   V A EC ECHQ £

8.30-22.00; closed Sunday (open on Sundays in December)

AUCHAN
Beer, wine and spirits
A huge hypermarket geared to English customers

Centre Commercial Auchan
Route Nationale 42
62200 St-Martin-Boulogne

On the main road out towards St-Omer
Tel: 21 92 06 00

Large car-park
English spoken
Wines on promotion may be tasted

Huge numbers of English tourists come here to buy their wine -
in fact 70% of sales are to the English. Most of the signs are in

English and there are plenty of people working in the shop who speak English. The shop itself is within a huge complex, and has one of the largest selections of drink I have ever seen under one roof. You can ask for help from Jacques Bigote, the wine Adviser who is very knowledgeable and will offer advice. Many of the products are geared to British visitors, with large bottles of Piat d'Or and German wine. There are 'Animateurs' shouting out special offers, and people giving out free samples to taste. As with all French supermarkets and hypermarkets, look out for promotions. Rock-bottom prices are available, which makes beers, aperitifs and spirits a good bet, but taste before buying wine in significant quantities.

MEDIUM-SIZED SHOP BOULOGNE A V EC EC

09.00-12.15 and 14.00-19.00, Tuesday to Saturday

CAVE PAUL HERPE
Wines and a few spirits
A fantastic place to discover the wines from Languedoc

---

85 rue Pasteur
62200 St-Martin-Boulogne
Boulogne-sur-Mer

Just off the RN42 towards St-Omer
Tel: 21 31 07 15

Adequate on-street parking
A little English spoken
All en Vrac wines may be tasted, plus some of the bottles

This is the sort of place that does not exist in the UK and is very exciting for British visitors to France. Cave Paul Herpe is a small chain of shops which specializes in the wines of Languedoc, most of which come from their own vineyards. They include familiar names such as Minervois, Fitou, Corbières and La Clape, but with a choice of wines from different estates and different vintages in each appellation. The overall choice of wine is fairly small but if you like full-bodied red wines from the south there is excellent value for money. What might be most attractive to buyers from the UK is the large choice of wines en Vrac. You can buy various sorts of containers; a good-quality reusable 15-litre air-tight box with a tap (in which the wine will keep for three months) will set you back 80 F which is much less than the equivalent packaging price cost you pay for wine in bottles. The wines themselves range from 8 to 30 F a litre. In addition to the still wines, there is a choice of sweet fortified Muscats from Banyuls and Rivesaltes (a couple of these are also en Vrac), and a sparkling Blanquette de Limoux at 36 F. M. Boulanger in the Boulogne shop was very friendly and helpful.

SMALL SHOP   BOULOGNE   A V £

10.00-19.30, every day

THE GRAPE SHOP
Wine only
An excellent English style wine shop

85-87 Rue Victor Hugo
62200 Boulogne-sur-Mer

In the centre of town, just back from the quayside
Tel: 21 33 93 30

Free underground car-park next door
All staff speak English
Extensive tasting

One of two shops (see entry below)

Large Shop Boulogne A V £

09.30-09.30, every day while SeaCat is running;
10.00-19.30 at other times

THE GRAPE SHOP
Wine only
A larger version of other Grape Shops

Gare Maritime
62200 Boulogne-sur-Mer

Just beside the SeaCat terminal
Tel: 21 30 16 17 (shop), 21 30 23 00 (office)

Plenty of parking space by shop
All staff speak English
Extensive tasting possible

Walk into either branch of The Grape Shop and you could be visiting a good branch of Wine Rack or Oddbins in the UK. You have a similar standard of quality but with prices around £1.50-£2.50 less per bottle. The savings on champagnes may be even greater. The list is constantly changing but everything in the shop has the stamp of quality and the helpful and friendly staff will guide you through the extensive range. If you are left with any doubts you will be able to taste anything you intend to buy in reasonable quantity. The number and quality of non-French wines is exceptional by the standards of wine shops in France, and includes Australians from Penfolds, Lindemans and Wolf Blass; Cooks and Montana from New Zealand; and Concha Y Toro from Chile. The range of French wines is also very large and well chosen, starting at around 15 F for Côtes de Gascogne white and Catalane Chardonnay. Although most areas are well represented, The Grape Shop specializes in champagnes. Look out in particular for the Gardet (95 F) and the Maurice Lassalle at a mere 69 F. The one reservation I have about this shop is that its very Englishness takes away some of the excitement and confusion of being in France.

LARGE WAREHOUSE   BOULOGNE   A V EC £ EC

09.00-12.00 and 14.30-19.00; closed Tuesday and Sunday

LE CHAIS
Wines, beers and spirits
A good large shop covering most needs

rue des Deux Ponts
Quartier Brequerecque
62200 Boulogne-sur-Mer

Tel: 21 31 65 42

Easy parking
English spoken
Many wines may be tasted

This is the same company as Le Chais described in the Calais section. The Boulogne branch is bigger and the manager Vincent Thoret claimed it is more upmarket. It certainly has a larger selection of wines and most notably some wines en Vrac. This branch is less well laid out than in Calais, and seemed to be busier, probably because the competition is less stiff in Boulogne. Most of the wines can be tasted - a huge advantage over other similar stores. For more details of Le Chais, see the Calais section.

There are also three branches of the shop **Les Vins de France** in Boulogne. This is part of the same chain as Le Chais, but has a much smaller range and is slightly more expensive. The shops are in central Boulogne, at:

11 rue Nationale, Tel. 21 30 51 00;
4 rue Lille, Tel. 21 80 55 96; and
28 rue de Brequereque, Tel. 21 80 55 96

SUPERMARKET BOULOGNE A V £ EC ECHQ

09.00-20.00, Monday to Saturday

PG
Good range of wines, beers and spirits
Very civilized superior supermarket

Centre Commercial Liane
boulevard Danou
62200 Boulogne-sur-Mer

Central Boulogne
Tel: 21 30 43 67

Large car-park
English spoken
Tasting possible

PG is a chain of supermarkets which have a particularly well-laid-out, attractive range of wines. They are not terribly big, certainly without the range of the hypermarkets, but what there is has been thoughtfully chosen and displayed in a way that can help to make shopping a less frustrating experience. PG are well geared to British customers, with a lot of information in English and many English speakers on hand. They also stock a range of drinks which are popular with British customers, such as Mateus Rosé and Piat d'Or. There is the fairly usual range of French supermarket cheapies, with the likes of Côtes du Ventoux, Bergerac, Cahors and Vin de Pays for between 10 and 20 F. There is also some good cheap Alsace for under 25 F and plenty of Loire red and white. The unusual thing about PG is that they have a separate section called La Cave, where there is a selection of very good quality wine from all over France. Here you find some excellent Cru Bourgeois and other Bordeaux in the 30-60 F range, and good Burgundy and Beaujolais from reliable producers such as Mommesin and Bouchard Père et Fils. The prices are all fairly reasonable. There is a good range of beers with a well presented selection from Belgium. As with the fine wines there is plenty of written information (in French) to help you choose. The prices of big-selling international brands of beers are a little higher than in hypermarkets and high-turnover warehouse shops though. As far as the spirits go, look out for the Armagnacs, as big savings are to be made here. The best value was the Pallas 3* at 69 F 95.

There are other branches of PG in Boulogne-sur-Mer at:
Boulevard Danou, Tel. 21 30 43 67;
80 rue Calonne, Tel. 21 80 43 67.
And in St-Martin-Boulogne at:
route Calais, Tel. 21 31 44 44;
route Paris, Tel. 21 91 02 55.

SMALL DRIVE-IN   SAMER   A V EC

09.00-12.00, Monday to Saturday

LES CAVES SAINT-JACQUES
Fairly small range of beers, wines and spirits
No-frills local drive-in shop

---

147 rue des Desvres
62830 Samer

On the D215
Tel: 21 83 14 45

Not easy to park near shop but there is a drive-in facility
Minimal English spoken
Tasting possible

This is not a place you would wander far out of your way for but nevertheless a shop where you could easily stock up on cheap wine, beer and the odd bottle of spirits to take home. The beers are mainly cheap, local French bières blondes and brunes. The wines start at about 10 Francs for VDP and there is a good choice for under 40 Francs. There are about ten red Bordeaux in that category which look good value, and a selection of the usual good value wines from the Loire, Alsace and the south. Before buying these in any quantity, however, you would want to taste them first, which you should be able to do in this shop. There are a few champagnes which include some familiar Grandes Marques, and the good value Eugenie Bézard at 69 F 95. Les Caves Saint-Jacques stocks a fairly standard range of fortified wines, aperitifs and spirits.

SMALL WAREHOUSE   ETAPLES   A V EC

09.00-12.00 and 14.00-18.30; closed Sunday and Monday

DRINKS AUTO BOISSONS
Wines, a few beers, usual spirits
A local drive-in drink shop

702 avenue d'Etaples
Trepeid
62630 Etaples

On the main road to Berck, just outside Etaples
Tel: 21 94 68 98

Private car-park
Very limited English spoken
En Vrac wines and for large sales of other wines

This is the place where the locals come to stock up with everyday drinking wines. Some of the wines they sell are very cheap with Bordeaux starting at around 12 F 50, Vacqueyras at 18 F, and Côtes de Ventoux at 11 F 20. Also worth checking out are the several wines en Vrac starting at 7 F/litre for Vin de Table, with a Merlot at 10 F /litre, a Côtes de Roussillon at 11 F/litre, and going up to 18 F/litre for Premières Côtes de Blaye. They sell good-quality 10-litre reusable containers which will keep the wine for up to three months. There is a white wine available en Vrac but be warned to steer clear. White wine is much more sensitive and will not keep well in these conditions. There are a few spirits and some beers. Unfortunately most of the beers are sold in returnable cases and will therefore not be of interest.

SUPERMARKET   ETAPLES   A V EC

09.00-20.00, Monday to Saturday

PG
Good range of beer, wines and spirits
Very civilized superior supermarket

route Boulogne
62630 Etaples

On the D940
Tel: 21 84 19 20

Large car-park
Some English spoken
Tasting possible

See comment for PG in Boulogne

MEDIUM-SIZED SHOP   LE TOUQUET   £ A V EC ECHQ

09.00-12.00 and 15.00-19.00; closed Wednesday and Sunday

LE CHAIS
Wines, beers and spirits
A good all-round shop

71 rue de Londres
62520 Le Touquet

In centre of Le Touquet
Tel: 21 05 59 83

Parking on street a short distance away
English spoken
No tasting

This is the same company as Le Chais which is described in the
Calais section and the Boulogne section above. This branch is

much smaller, with less choice but from the same list and at similar prices. There are only a handful of beers sold here, and it is much more of a traditional, relaxed, provincial wine shop.

SMALL WAREHOUSE   NR. ETAPLES   AVEC

09.00-19.00, Tuesday to Saturday

BOISSONS SERVICE
Wines, beers, soft drinks
A local drive-in drink shop

34 route Nationale 39
62170 Enocq

Half-way between Etaples and Montreuil on N39
Tel: 21 86 29 11

Easy parking outside shop
Minimal English spoken
Cheaper wines may be tasted if purchase is intended

Another supplier of everyday drinking wine and beer for the locals. No wine en Vrac here but there is a reasonable selection of local beer, a couple of ciders for around 10 F (a 75cl bottle) and lots of cheap wine. It is worth looking out for some very cheap Vin de Pays de L'Hérault and AOC Bordeaux. They have a reasonable selection of most of the other major regions but not many whites apart from Muscadet and wines from Alsace. The quality is generally the equivalent of a French supermarket but the advantage of these small warehouse shops is that you can get advice and taste some of the wines, which is definitely advisable if you are buying a large quantity.

MEDIUM-SIZED SHOP   BERCK-PLAGE   A V EC ECHQ

09.00-12.15 and 14.00-19.00, Tuesday to Saturday

CAVE PAUL HERPE
Wines and a few spirits
A fantastic place to discover the wines from Languedoc

450 rue de l'Impératrice
62600 Berck-Plage

On the main road into town from Le Touquet
Tel: 21 84 10 45

Adequate on-street parking
A little English spoken
All en Vrac wines and some bottles may be tasted with sales

Cave Paul Herpe has a good choice of wines from Languedoc and is described in the Boulogne section.

Medium-sized Shop   Berck-Plage   A V EC

10.00-12.00 and 15.00-19.00

LA VIGNOTHÈQUE
Wine and spirits
A reasonable shop where you might pick up the odd bottle

102 rue de L'Imperatrice
62600 Berck-Plage

On the main road into town from Le Touquet
Tel: 21 84 87 77

Easy on-street parking
Some English spoken
Tasting possible with prospect of large sales

M. Denneulin who runs the Vignothèque has a fairly classic range of French wines including Grand Cru Classe dating back to 1929. The best bets are red Bordeaux coming from small producers with whom he has built up a relationship over the last fifteen years, which are priced in the 25-50 F range. Apart from that there are some good quality but quite highly priced regional ACs, such as Cahors and Côtes de Marmandais, some fairly expensive Burgundy from good producers, and a fairly small selection from the other major French regions. The champagnes are well-chosen: an Etienne Doué at 78 F and a Simart Premier Cru at 86 F. There are a few spirits, including some old Cognacs and Armagnacs which have been chosen for their individuality rather than their price. Unusually for a French-run shop, there are a couple of Australian and Chilean wines.

HOTEL, RESTAURANT AND SHOP
MONTREUIL   A V EC AMEX ECHQ £

08.00-22.00, every day

LES HAUTS DE MONTREUIL
Wines, spirits and a few speciality beers
A place to visit and marvel

21-23 rue Pierre Ledent
62179 Montreuil-sur-Mer

On the main road through the centre of Montreuil
Tel: 21 81 95 92

Private car-park
English spoken
Tasting possible

M. Gantiez who runs Les Hauts de Montreuil is a character who is literally larger than life. To say that he gets job satisfaction from running his 16th-century hotel with restaurant and wine cellars would be an understatement. The enthusiasm with which he showed me his collection of top growth wines, calling out the value of each, was that of a proud parent presenting his children. The first cellar contains the fine wines and maturing cheese. I nearly passed out when I smelt the cheese which he religiously washes in beer to encourage a flavour-enhancing mould. The second cellar is more down to earth and contains a pleasant if small collection of wines, speciality beers and spirits. There is also a selection of food delicacies: sausages hanging from the ceiling, foie gras and jams, all nicely presented and suitable as presents. There are no fantastic bargains but the atmosphere is very warm and M. Gantiez is sure to offer something to taste while he lectures you on some aspect of French viticulture or gastronomy. The hotel looked great (double rooms from 350 F) and the restaurant menu was very inviting. This is the sort of place in which to spend the money you save from crossing the Channel to buy drink.

LARGE WINE SHOP   MONTREUIL-SUR-MER
A V EC AMEX ECHQ £

08.00-12.30 and 14.00-19.00, Monday to Saturday; 10.00-to 12.30 and 15.30-19.00, Sundays and holidays

VINOPHILIE
Wines and spirits
A very smart wine shop

2 rue Grand Sermon
62170 Montreuil

In the centre of Montreuil
Tel: 21 06 01 54

Small car-park
A little English spoken
Tasting possible on some wines

Vinophilie is a very smart shop with a lot of expensive wine. It seems quite incongruous therefore to see the range of wines en Vrac in the centre of the shop which start at 6 F a litre. This is one of the joys of buying wine in France, that even in a place like this you need feel no shame at choosing a bottle of Vin de Pays or a simple Bordeaux. Some of the wines are very good value, the house champagne is 63 F, and there was some cheap Côtes de Blaye and Côtes de Castillon. Few of the more expensive wines will be cheaper than in the UK, but you can enjoy looking. There is also a smart range of spirits including Cognacs, Armagnacs and whiskys, and it is worth looking out for the good selection of the local speciality Genièvre. Good discounts are negotiable on buying a large quantity.

WINE CELLAR AND SHOP   BEAURAINVILLE
A V EC ECHQ

09.00-12.00 and 14.00-19.00, Monday to Saturday

LES CAVES ST-MARTIN
Wines only
A huge cellar filled with interesting wine

1 rue Chateau
62990 Beaurainville

Well signposted once in Beaurainville
Tel: 21 90 32 98

Easy on-street parking
A little English spoken
Tasting possible on most wines for serious purchase

Not far from Loison is this atmospheric, large cellar wine shop where you get the feeling that stock inventories are fairly rare events. I saw a good selection covering all the regions of France, with prices from 10 F for basic Bordeaux up to 1000 F for Grand Cru Classé. The shop was particularly strong on good-quality wines in the 30-40 F range, although there was a fair choice of wines cheaper than that. As with most outlets in this part of France, Bordeaux is the favoured region. Caves St. Martin has a mixture of wines from négociants and wines from small producers. A Vin de Table and a Côtes de Bourg are bottled on site. The large producers are all well known and reliable: names such as Drouhin and Bichot from Burgundy and Jaboulet and Delas from the Rhône, whose wines are unlikely to be much cheaper than in the UK. The Alsace wines from producers Sparr and Scherer are significantly cheaper, with several available for under 30 F. There was a good promotion on when I visited and significant savings for bulk buys. There is a fairly standard range of spirits. This shop is great if you enjoy browsing, not too stuffy, and the Château Pétrus rubs shoulders with the Vins de Table.

PRODUCER WITH SHOP LOISON-SUR-CRÉQUOISE A V EC ECHQ

09.00-12.00 and 14.00-19.00, Monday to Saturday; open Sunday in season

LA MAISON DU PERLÉ
Cider, Perle and Eau de Vie de Cidre
An artisanale drink producer

50 rue Principale
62990 Loison-Sur-Crequoise

On the main road in Loison-sur-Créquoise
Tel: 21 81 30 85

Private car-park
English spoken
Tasting possible

This is perhaps more of a destination for tourists than a place to buy drink. La Maison du Perlé is a small family run producer of Perlé, Cider and Eau de Vie de Cidre (cider spirit). Perlé is a sparkling aperitif wine made out of redcurrants or raspberries and costs 66 F a bottle. The cider is genuine unpasteurized farm cider which starts off slightly sweet, but after a few months the active yeast in the bottle will have converted all the sugar into alcohol. The cider will then be dry, more alcoholic and fizzier. They also sell a spirit made from distilled cider for 140 F. Aside from these alcoholic drinks, there are a number of other touristy things for sale such as jams, chocolates and foie gras. M. and Mme Delobel arrange tours showing how each product is made, finishing up with a sampling of the various products. The cost is currently 12 F per person. The countryside around is very pretty and this is a good place for a family visit.

WINE CELLAR WITH SHOP   FRESSIN
A V EC ECHQ

08.30-12.30 and 13.30-19.00

LES CAVES DU VIEUX CHAI
Wine and spirits
A terrific place to visit and buy wine

20 Grand Rue
Fressin
62140 Hesdin
On the main street through Fressin
Tel: 21 90 61 43
Plenty of parking available near the shop
English spoken
Many wines available for tasting

This is the nearest thing to actually visiting a wine producer in situ. The current generation of the Glacon family are the third in a line of négociant-éleveurs. This means that they buy wines, and mature a number of them in oak barrels before bottling them. Large numbers of fine wine are stored in their 600 m^2 cellar, including a small section of very fine wines; Château Yquem, Château Lafitte, etc. The main cellar houses the bulk of these wines which are mainly from Bordeaux with a choice of vintages from selected Châteaux. There are good wines from Côtes de Bourg, Premières Côtes de Bordeaux and Fronsac for under 30 F which can all be tasted, and plenty of Cru Bourgeois and others more expensive. Otherwise, there was a reasonable selection of wines from the Loire and Alsace (the reliable but cheap Cave de Sigolsheim) and a few from Burgundy and the Rhone. The Paul Glacon house champagne was 76 F and there was also some good value Saumur and Blanquette de Limoux. There is also a selection of cheap VDP de Var and Côteaux de Tricastin in bottles and in large boxes. The spirits on sale consist of a few good-quality Eaux de Vie d'Alsace, brandy and Armagnac. This is a great place to buy wine; a good selection priced with something for everyone, plenty available to taste, good discounts on quantity, and friendly members of the Glacon family to help you choose.

MEDIUM-SIZED SHOP   HESDIN   A V ECHQ

08.00-12.30 and 13.45-18.00, Monday to Saturday

THE WINE SOCIETY
Wines and spirits
A shop for Wine Society members only

c/o Distilleries Rhyssen
rue Fressin
62140 Hesdin

Just next to the central square in Hesdin
Tel: 21 81 61 70

Easy on-street parking
English spoken
One or two wines per week on tasting

The Wine Society is a co-operative, whose aim is to offer its members good value rather than maximize profit. Membership involves a one-off payment of £20 and allows the members to buy wines from its list which covers most of the major wine-producing regions of the world. The wines are carefully selected, and quality and value for money are very reliable. The shop in Hesdin sells the sixty most popular wines at a reduction from the UK prices. The best savings are on the cheap sparkling wines, otherwise they are somewhere in the region of 50p to £1.20 per bottle. In addition to a cross-section of French wines, many on offer at Hesdin are non-French and are rarely seen in French shops, including Australian, Italian and Spanish. There are also a few ports, sherrys and whiskys, a gin and a vodka. Plans are afoot to sell beer in 1995. You can join the Wine Society at the shop in Hesdin.

The Wine Society's landlords, Distilleries Rhyssen, have a separate shop, selling a small and typically French selection of wines which includes Bordeaux, Burgundy, Champagnes and pastis. The wines are fairly cheap but less reliable in quality than those of their tennant.

SMART SHOP PLUS DRIVE-IN   ST-POL-SUR-TERNOISE   A V EC ECHQ

08.30-12.30 and 14.00-19.00, Tuesday to Saturday

CAVES ST-POLNOISE
Beer, wine and spirits
A superior drive-in drink shop

---

2 rue de Frevent
62130 Saint-Pol-sur-Ternoise

Almost opposite the town hall
Tel: 21 03 09 85

On street outside, but drive-in possible
Minimal English spoken
Tasting possible but not encouraged

The shop owned and run by M. and Mme Demont was in the process of being refurbished when I visited. It is split into two parts with different entrances: one for beers, minerals and cheap wines, and the other for fine wines and spirits. There is a good selection of French and Belgian beers, and a long list of wines, ranging from VDP and lesser ACs from 10 F to Bordeaux Grand Cru Classe. There are wines available from every part of France and at every price. They usually have promotions which are worth taking advantage of; when I visited there was some good AC Bordeaux, Médoc, Fronsac and Côtes de Bourg all available for under 30 F, and a red Côtes de Duras 93 for 14 F. The shop has a selection of cheap 3-litre disposable bag-in-the-boxes, but Mme Demont reckoned they would only survive for a month. The selection of spirits is good and includes 14 different varieties of Calvados and 20 Armagnacs. This is a busy friendly place, although the delivery man wasn't keen to encourage English customers because he thought he would have to start delivering in Britain.

SMALL SHOP   ARRAS   A V EC

9.30-13.00 and 14.00-19.30; closed Sunday, and Monday a.m.

LE CELLIER DES BIÈRES DE BELGIQUE
Beer
A specialist Belgian beer shop

30 rue de la Taillerie
62000 Arras

Between the place des Héros and the Grande Place in the centre of town
Tel: 21 51 34 94

Pay-zone parking
English spoken
Tasting on selected days

Le Cellier is a small shop in a lovely location in the centre of Arras which just sells Belgian beer. Every Belgian beer you can think of is here, including Trappists, Lambics and abbey beers. The list includes amongst others Namur White, Hoegaarden, Brigand, Bush, Chimay, Duvel, Gueuze, Julius, Kwak, Leffe, Morte Subite, Orval, Saint-Sixtus and Triple Moine. Many of the beers are sold in bottles of different sizes up to 9-litre magnums. M. and Mme Verdière who run the shop organize tastings from time to time, so it is worth phoning up to check if one is coming up. M. Verdière will also be happy to offer advice in English if you are baffled by the array of bottles.

SMALL SHOP   ARRAS   A V EC

08.30-12.30 and 14.00-19.00, Tuesday to Saturday

JAILLOUX-BILOT
300 wines, 300 spirits and a few beers
A small dusty wine shop

2 rue Pasteur
62000 Arras

Near the Grande Place in the centre of Arras
Tel: 21 51 28 48

Parking difficult
No English spoken
No tasting

This small, old-fashioned city-centre shop is not somewhere you would stock up, but a place you might pick up one or two curiosities. The shop has some cheap wine, with a Vin de Table Cuvée de la Maison at 11 F 50, a few reasonable Bordeaux reds, and some cheap rosés. Unfortunately there is no tasting and it might be a bit risky buying these blind. There are some good-quality Burgundies and Rhônes but the prices are not particularly good. The shop also sells unusual Greek, Portuguese and Spanish wines which are rarely seen in France. I was intrigued by a local Arras beer called Atrebate which was 15 F for a large bottle. The collection of Cognac, Calvados, Armagnac, Eaux de Vie and the local speciality Genièvre de Houlle was good and varied. The dusty, unkempt atmosphere of the place gives you the feeling that if you root around for long enough you might find a forgotten bargain hidden away somewhere.

MEDIUM-SIZED SHOP   ARRAS   AMEX A V EC

9.00-12.00 and 14.00-19.00, Monday afternoon to Saturday

MILLÉSIMES
Wines and spirits
A smart city-centre shop

46 rue des 3 Visages
62000 Arras

Central Arras
Tel: 21 07 64 63

Pay-zone parking
Little English spoken
No tasting

Millésimes is a smart shop in the centre of Arras. The shop has an expensive feel, and you get the impression that if you browse for long the shop assistant will keep asking if he can help you. Many shops in France seem to use the Guide Hachette to select their wines and this is one of them. The Guide Hachette is the French wine bible, and is apparently a reliable judge of quality. I didn't spot many bargains in this place, although there were a few country wines and lesser Bordeaux which were cheaper than they would be in Britain. In addition to the wines there is a good selection of Armagnacs and Calvados that you wouldn't find back home, but nothing really shouted 'BUY ME'.

LARGE SHOP   ARRAS   A V ECHQ

09.00-12.00, Tuesday to Saturday

ROQUILLAS
Large range of wines and spirits
A good large wine shop with bargains available

3 rue d'Archicourt
62000 Arras

Off the Arras ring road towards the suburb of Archicourt
Tel: 21 23 00 43

Easy parking on street
Limited English spoken
Restricted tasting possible

Roquillas seems to be the biggest and best place to buy wine in Arras. The wines in the shop betray the regional bias, with plenty of full-bodied red wine especially from Bordeaux, and not a lot of white. The shop is quite large with plenty to browse through. The staff were not terribly friendly or helpful, but this might have had something to do with it being the pre-Christmas period, and they were very keen to sort out their Christmas promotions. The shop is quite smart with a high proportion of fairly expensive Burgundy, Bordeaux and Rhone. There was, however, a good selection of wines under 30 F. These included lesser Bordeaux ACs, some Vins de Pays and southern ACs such as Fitou, Corbières and Côtes de Duras. The Domaine de Montmarin Vin de Pays des Côtes de Thongue Syrah was excellent value at 18 F. Roquillas also sells a number of wines en Vrac, by the litre or in 11-, 22- or 32-litre vacuum packs. They have very reasonably priced own-label wines: a Vin de Table, an AC Bordeaux, a Côtes de Bourg, a Côtes du Rhône, and a Muscat de Rivesaltes. These may be tasted, and if you find one you like they constitute excellent value. The shop stocks most other standard French wines including a large selection of not terribly cheap champagnes. They also sell a lot of interesting-looking rare old Calvados, Armagnacs and Eaux de Vie. Look out for promotions, when I visited they had Beaujolais Cru on special offer.

Route 3

This route carries on in an easterly direction beyond Calais along the A16 to Dunkerque. It then splits with one path taking the A25 south-east via Bergues and Poperinge to Lille and another continuing along the coast into Belgium via Veurne and Oostende, finally turning inland to Bruges.

Dunkerque is the first place on this route, 40km east of Calais. There are good places for shopping in Dunkerque, with plenty of shops and hypermarkets, but otherwise it is not the most attractive of cities. This is hardly surprising considering its history of being bombarded and fought over. There are a few good museums, an aquarium and most of the other amenities of a large town. Information is available at the tourist office at **4 place Charles Valentin, 59240 Dunkerque, Tel. 28 26 27 89. Le XIXème Siècle** (Dix-neuvième Siècle), **1 place de La Gare, Tel. 28 66 79 28** is a good, reasonably priced place to stay near the railway station. If you fancy a view try the comfortable but ugly and soulless, multi-storey **Altea Reuze, 2 rue Jean Jaurès, Tel. 28 59 11 11** in the centre of town, where double rooms with en-suite bathroom start at 300 F. It is easy to find a reasonable-looking menu in town.

Bergues is an atmospheric small, walled town built in typical Flemish style. The architecture is lovely and an attractive canal runs through the town which adds to its charm. There are two good places to stay, and being only 10km from Dunkerque makes it a much preferable overnight stop. The **Hôtel du Commerce, Contour de l'êglise, Tel. 28 68 60 37** is informal and comfortable with double rooms starting at 300F. Next door is the **Au Tonnelier, 4 rue des Monts de Piete, Tel. 28 68 70 05**, which is a little more formal but similarly priced. Au Tonnelier has an excellent menu, but there are plenty of other attractive places to eat within walking distance. **Le Cornet d'Or, 26 rue Espagnole, Tel. 28 68 66 27** is excellent.

Lille is actually a little more than an hour's drive from the Tunnel, but it is included because it is a major city full of interest. It is a place to come for a little sophisticated city life; there is excellent shopping, an attractive old town, a fine selection of restaurants and cafés, museums, theatre and opera, etc. Of particular interest is the **Museum of Fine Arts, place de la République, Tel. 20 57 01 84** which is the biggest museum in France after the Louvre, and the **Museum of Charles de Gaulle, Tel. 9 rue Princesse, 20 31 96 03**. Full details of all Lille's attractions are available at The **Tourist Information, place Rihour, BP 205, Tel 20 30 81 00**. There are numerous places to stay and eat. **Hôtel de la Treille, 7-9 place Louise de Bettignies, Tel. 20 06 66 07**, is central and very comfortable. Double rooms with en-suite bathroom start from 370 F. Cheaper and smaller with a little more character is the **Hôtel Breughel, 5 parvis St-Maurice, Tel. 20 06 06 69**. Lille is extremely well endowed with good cafés, restaurants, brasseries and bars, and eating out is definitely one of the attractions of the visit.

Back along the coast road from Dunkerque in the direction of Oostende, the first place you get to across the Belgian border is **Veurne**. It is another attractive town with many fine early 17th-century buildings built in the Flemish style. There is a picturesque central square lined with cafés serving delicious snacks, and an excellent range of Belgian beers. The best place to stay is the very comfortable **Hôtel Croonhof, 9 Noordstraat, Tel. (058) 31 31 28** where double rooms cost 2,200 BF. There are plenty of good places around to eat the local specialities of boudin (sausages), rabbit, salmon and trout.

Much of the Belgian coast is a seamless stretch of sandy beach, lined with apartment blocks. Places such as **Nieuwpoort** and **Middelkerke** are not major attractions, but are good summer resorts with all the essential holiday amenities. **Oostende** stands out on the coast. It is a relaxed, slightly scruffy port with a pleasant atmosphere and plenty to do. For information about places to stay along the coast, contact the **Tourist Information** in Oostende at **Monacoplein 2, 8400 Oostende, Tel. (059) 70 11 99**, or in Middelkerke at **V.V.V, J. Casselaan 4, 8430 Middelkerke, Tel. (059) 30 03 68**, or in Nieuwpoort at **Stadhuis, Marktplein 7, 8620**

Nieuwpoort, Tel. (058 23 55 94.

Bruges may also be slightly outside the one-hour range from the Tunnel, but it is included in this book because it is a real gem. Few cities in Europe can match its character and charm. There are plenty of sights: the Grotemarkt, St. Saviour's Cathedral and the Bonifacius Bridge amongst them, but it is just by wandering through the enchanting maze of alley-ways criss-crossed by canals that you experience the real attraction of Bruges. Eating out is an important part of any visit to Bruges because the food is excellent. There is plenty of choice everywhere but you should have at least one meal on the Grotemarkt (central square). Although somewhat touristy, the surroundings make for a wonderful experience. Away from the restaurants there are two gastronomic specialities which deserve special mention: chocolates and beer. The local chocolates are amazing, and available almost at every street corner. Don't leave town without trying them or the fabulous beer, numerous varieties of which are sold at the many atmospheric bars and cafés throughout the city. A cheap, basic place to stay is the **Singe d'Or, 't Zand 18, 8000 Bruges, Tel. (050) 33 48 48)** above an inviting cafe, with double rooms from 1,500 BF. If you are looking for somewhere smarter, try the **Pandhotel, Pandreitje 12, Tel. (050) 34 06 66** which is stylish and comfortable. Double rooms start at 5,000 BF. Information is available from the **Tourist Office, Burg 11, 8000 Bruges, Tel. (050) 44 86 86**.

HYPERMARKET DUNKERQUE £ A V EC ECHQ

09.00-22.00, Monday to Saturday; open on Sunday in December

AUCHAN
Large range of wines, beers and spirits
This is a huge hypermarket

avenue Ancien Village
Off Route Nationale 40
59760 Grand Synthe

In Grand Synthe to the west of central Dunkerque
Tel: 28 27 99 99

Large car-park
English spoken
Tasting on occasional promotions

See entry for Auchan in Boulogne.

SMALL SHOP DUNKERQUE A V EC ECHQ

10.00-19.00; closed Sunday and Monday (except in December)

LA BORDELAISE DU NORD
Smallish range of expensive wines, whiskies and brandies
Few bargains relative to the UK

65-67 Boulevard Alexandre III
59140 Dunkerque

Central Dunkerque next to Cadovino
Tel: 28 66 00 41

Reasonable on-street parking
English spoken
Tasting possible but not encouraged

This is a very smart shop located next door to Cadovino. It is run
by M. Cuisinier whose approach couldn't be more different from

that of his neighbour, in that everything he sells comes from a big producer of high reputation. There are plenty of Grand Cru Classé Clarets, Yquem, Pétrus, Burgundies from Drouhin, big-name champagnes, and famous Cognacs and Armagnacs. M. Cuisinier does not keep a consistent stock but buys in small quantities when he finds something he likes the look of. Unfortunately few of the wines he sells are likely to be cheaper here than in the UK and you will probably leave the shop empty-handed. As the owner said with a good-natured shrug of the shoulders, many of the English customers who come in say they are 'just looking'.

Small shop   Dunkerque   A V EC ECHQ

09.30-12.00 and 14.30-19.00, closed on Sunday and Monday

CADOVINO
A fairly small range of wines and a few spirits
A shop for buying gifts or a one-off bottle

Angle 2
rue Dampierre
59140 Dunkerque

Central Dunkerque
Tel: 28 21 00 99

Reasonable on-street parking
A little English spoken
Tasting possible but not encouraged

Formerly called Tastevins de Flandre, this shop is run by Bernard Messiaen and his wife Evelyne. Although quite a small shop without a huge range, Bernard takes his wines very seriously and carefully selects traditionally made wines from small independent producers, which genuinely reflect the style of the region. The wines and the few spirits all come from the major areas of production in France. Don't expect to find bargain-basement prices because this is a place which concentrates on exclusivity and quality. There is a large range of gift boxes and packs, so although you probably won't fill your car here you could well find an interesting one-off bottle to keep for yourself or to give as a present.

HYPERMARKET DUNKERQUE A V EC ECHQ

08.30-21.00, Monday to Saturday

CARREFOUR
Large range of wines, beers and spirits
A good large supermarket with few British customers

Centre Commercial St-Pol
59430 St-Pol-sur-Mer

In St-Pol-sur-Mer
Tel: 28 64 79 11

Large car-park
Limited English spoken
No tasting

This is a very good large hypermarket which for some reason is ignored by most British visitors. The drinks selection seems to reflect this with far fewer British favourites than the nearby Auchan. Perhaps, because of this, it is a good place to visit, with plenty of French wines in all styles and at all prices. The most interesting thing about the Carrefour selection is the range of own-label wines which includes very reasonably priced Côtes de Bourg at 18 F, Bordeaux Blanc Sec at 13 F 50, Bordeaux red for 16 F, Muscadet for 16 F, Médoc for 22 F 50, and others. Beers here are well priced but you will find fewer of the cans popular with British customers. Other good buys include an own-label Cognac for 65 F and an Armagnac for 66 F. Carrefour looks a good all-round choice to stock up on bulk.

Large Warehouse   Dunkerque (Ferry Port)   A V £ EC ECHQ

08.00-24.00, Monday to Friday; and 10.00-18.00, Saturday and Sunday

CASH AND CARRY
Wines, beers and spirits
A warehouse shop, not very good value

route du Petit Denna
59270 Loon Plage

Just by Dunkerque Ferry Port
Tel: 28 27 35 70

Large car-park
English spoken
Selected wines may be tasted

This is a large Cash and Carry warehouse near to the Ferry Terminal - the sort of place that looks like it will have many bargains at discount prices but in fact you can find better value elsewhere. They do not keep a regular list of wines so stock will vary quite a lot over time. The shop attempts to cater for British customers with things such as Piesporter Michelsberg (similar to Liebfraumilch) at 16 F 50 and cases of beer. There is a full range of most wine styles, Belgian beers, standard lager beers and spirits, but prices are such that this shop is really only worth coming to on Sundays when the supermarkets in town are closed.

SMALL SHOP   DUNKERQUE   A V EC

09.00-12.00 and 14.00-19.00, Tuesday to Saturday

CAVE PAUL HERPE
Wines and a few spirits
Great for buying less well-known wines of Languedoc

208 rue de la République
59430 St-Pol-sur-Mer

On the main road through St-Pol-sur-Mer
Tel: 28 60 99 19

Car-park
Limited English spoken
Tasting possible

This is part of the chain of Cave Paul Herpe shops which are described fully in the Boulogne section in Chapter 16. Definitely worth a visit, this place has a good selection of wines en Vrac and other wines in bottle from the south.

Small shop   Dunkerque   A V EC

09.15-12.15, Monday afternoon to Saturday

CAVEAU SAINTE URSULE
Wines and a few speciality beers
An interesting place to buy wine

49 bis rue Marengo
59140 Dunkerque

In central Dunkerque
Tel: 28 21 17 03

Adequate on-street parking
Minimal English spoken
Wines en Vrac may be tasted

As with restaurants with a short menu there is something about a small shop with a limited range which inspires confidence. Each item has been selected carefully, the sales person knows what he is selling, and it is also much easier to choose. The only disadvantage is that you are likely to exhaust the choices if you come back regularly, but this is not going to be a problem for most visitors from abroad. At the Caveau Ste. Ursule you have a choice of seven wines en Vrac, ranging from a rosé from the Pays de Var at 8 F 70 to a Côtes de Bourg red at 17F. You can buy a plastic container here but the wine will need to be decanted into bottles. I was told that bottling was a simple and straightforward process that just involved having clean bottles and soaking the corks in the wine before pushing them in, but I am not entirely convinced. Otherwise there was a good range of reasonably priced wines including a little of everything: a Côtes du Ventoux at 12 F, Loire reds at 35 F and a range of Monmarthe champagnes including a Premier Cru, a rosé and a vintage all very reasonably priced.

SMALL WAREHOUSE DUNKERQUE A V EC

09.30-12.30 and 14.00-19.00, Tuesday to Saturday

CHAIS DE LA TRANSAT
A good range of wines and spirits
A really pleasant atmosphere in which to buy wine

25 rue du Gouvernement
Quartier de la Citadelle
59140 Dunkerque

Central Dunkerque
Tel: 28 63 78 25

Easy parking on street
A little English spoken
Tasting not encouraged but possible with sales

If you enjoy a chat about wine, Eric Rassin who runs the Dunkerque branch of Chais de la Transat is very good company. This was one of my favourite shops: an excellent choice of carefully selected wines in most categories and from most French regions, a friendly laid-back atmosphere where you can browse at will and get plenty of sound advice. Chais de la Transat is a chain of five shops which arose from the demise of the Transat Steam Ship company which ran cruise ships like the SS France. The founders realized that this was a very marketable name which was associated with gastronomic excellence. The shop is very much aimed at providing high quality but there are plenty of own-label wines which are very good value. There are lots of famous names: good producers such as Guigal from the Rhône, and Jadot and Faively from Burgundy. There are spirits and fortified wines too; own-label Calvados and Pastis looked particularly appealing.

SUPERMARKET DUNKERQUE (FERRY PORT) A V EC ECHQ

09.00-20.00, Monday to Saturday

PG
Good range of wines, beers and spirits
Cheaper and better than the local competition

Zone d'Activités Commerciales
route de Gravelines
59279 Loon Plage

Near the Ferry Terminal
Tel: 28 27 37 69

Large car-park
Some English spoken
Tasting possible

For full details about PG supermarkets see the Boulogne section (Chapter 16). This place is very near the Ferry Terminal, cheaper and with a better range than either the shop in the Terminal or the Cash and Carry nearby. The range is not as good as in the large hypermarkets further into town, and beer and spirit prices are higher. The wine choice is very good and this is a laid-back environment in which to choose. There is a wine adviser here called Dominique who speaks English and will be glad to help you out.

SMALL SHOP   DUNKERQUE (FERRY PORT)
A V TC ECHQ £

08.00-13.15 and 14.30-20.00, Tuesday to Saturday and 12.00-20.00, Sunday and Monday

SALLY RETAIL
Wine, beer and a few spirits
Limited range of UK favourites

Terminal Ramsgate
Dunkerque Port Ouest
59279 Loon Plage

At the Sally Line Terminal
Tel: 28 27 35 44

Large car-park
English spoken
No tasting

A lot of the customers come to this shop straight off the ferry then turn straight round and head back to England, which is a pity because it isn't exactly a memorable shopping experience. The shop is geared entirely to the British customer, with a short list of cheap wines, beers and own-label spirits. If you want McEwans or Newcastle Brown this is the only place in Dunkerque to get it. There is also a Portacabin out in the car-park where you can load larger quantities straight on to the car. If you want anything other than cases of familiar beer I would get into the car and head into town.

DRIVE-IN BERGUES A V EC

08.30-12.15 and 14.00-18.45, Monday to Saturday

CLAUDE MEESEMACKER
Wines, beers and a few spirits
A friendly local French drive-in

28 rue du Port
59380 Bergues

In the centre of Bergues
Tel: 28 68 61 13

Easy parking
Limited English spoken
Tasting possible

This is a quite deceptive local drive-in shop because although there is relatively little on display there are large cellars underneath. The shop has a reasonable selection of cheaper wines, and the helpful assistant had a refreshingly honest approach to their varying degrees of merit. We were steered away from a Vin de Table at 5 F 70 which was apparently *degeulas* (not pleasant) but told that another one for only a few francs more was very buvable (drinkable). The choice of wines at the cheaper end is quite good: half a dozen wines en Vrac (although no containers), and the usual Muscadet, Côtes du Rhône, Beaujolais and the usual lesser Bordeaux. Although the shop was unremarkable and the selection a lot smaller than at hypermarkets, the prices are competitive and the service and possibility of tasting make it more likely that you will find what you are looking for. We received plenty of recommendations and warnings. The selection of Belgian beers was particularly good for this side of the border, including favourites such as Hoegaarden Grand Cru, Leffe and the delicious French 3 Monts. The prices for these were all very good.

DRIVE-IN   POPERINGE   FF FB ECHQ

10.00-12.00 and 14.00-17.00; closed Friday and Sunday

ABDIJ SINT SIXTUS
Beer
A unique place to buy beer

8640 Westvleteren
West Flanders

Well sign-posted from D948 near Poperinge
Tel: (057) 40 10 57

Drive-in
English spoken
Tasting in café next door

For the sheer novelty of the experience this place is unmissable.
The abbey is a Trappist monastery where three different types of
traditional unpasteurized beer are brewed. What you do is go
into the Café de Vrede to try out the three beers: the Special (6%
abv), the Extra (8% abv) and the Abbot (12% abv). You then go
next door to the drive-in beer shop and load your car up with as
many crates as you can pack in, aided by a friendly Trappist
monk. The beers come in unmarked bottles; you can only tell
which is which by the colour of the caps. The beer is remarkably
cheap, 600 BF for 24 bottles of Special, 700 BF for 24 Extra and 920
BF for 24 Abbot. A small deposit is paid for the wooden crates.
Genuine Sint Sixtus beer can only be bought here, other beer
labelled Sint Sixtus is available from shops but it is brewed elsewhere and is far inferior.

Medium-sized shop Poperinge £ FF FB ECHQ

08.00-12.00 and 13.00-20.00, every day

NOEL CUVELIER'S BEER SHOP
Beers, a few wines and spirits
A beer drinker's heaven

Abelestationsplein 30
8970 Poperinge
West Flanders

Just off the N28 between Poperinge and the A25. Very close to the French border
Tel: (057) 33 33 05

Large car-park
English spoken
No tasting

This place is wonderful. Noel Cuvelier, as friendly and garrulous a shop-keeper as you could ever meet, enthuses about his fabulous collection of over 300 different types of Belgian beer. He started off with an ordinary grocery store and only began selling beer to help a friend offload some unwanted stock. Now he has everything you have ever heard of and a lot more: Lambics, Gueuze, Trappists, White Beers, Dark Beers and Blond, by the bottle but cheaper by the case. The beers come in all shapes and sizes from 25cl up to 3-litre Jereboams and there are plenty of presentation gift packs to choose from. Each beer has its own special glass and Noel Cuvelier stocks a large number of these. The prices are very good, significantly cheaper than in Belgian supermarkets, much cheaper than in France and unbelievable by British standards: top-quality beers at 8% abv at the equivalent of 50-60p for a 33cl bottle. This shop is just over the Belgian border, and slightly out of the way, but definitely worth a special trip.

HYPERMARKET   LILLE   A V EC ECHQ

09.00-22.00 Monday to Saturday; open on Sunday in December

AUCHAN
Large range of wines, beers and spirits
Huge hypermarket

Centre Commercial Englos les Geants
59320 Englos

Just off the Lomme exit of the A25
Tel: 20 92 92 33

Large car-park
English spoken
Tasting on occasional promotions

This Auchan is conveniently situated just off the motorway to
Dunkerque. See entry for Auchan in Boulogne.

DRIVE-IN SHOP   LILLE   A V ECHQ

09.00-12.30 and 15.00-19.00, Monday to Saturday

CAVES MAITRE GEORGES
Wine, beer and spirits
A local drive-in drink store

---

98 bis rue Brule Maison
59000 Lille

In the south of Lille, off rue Solferino
Tel: 20 57 95 00

On-street parking or drive-in
A little English spoken
Current wines on tasting

This is a fairly typical French drive-in drink store specializing in
bulk sales. It is not worth going far out of your way to find it, but

the locals seem very happy to fill their cars up here. Aside from a fairly standard selection of French wines covering most price categories, and spirits, there are a lot of Belgian beers which are competitively priced for France (more expensive than in Belgium), including Gueuze, Kriek, Trappists, Hoegaarden and Rodenbach.

LARGE SHOP   LILLE   A V EC

09.00-20.00; closed Sunday and Monday morning

CAVES ROHART
Wine, beer and spirits
A smart city-centre shop with a large interesting range

66 rue Faidherbe
59800 Lille

On road connecting the Grande Place and the station
Tel: 20 06 29 92

City-centre parking
Some English spoken
No tasting

Caves Rohart is a cramped shop on three floors with a huge range of all kinds of wines, beers and spirits. This shop is quite smart, and gives you a feeling of quality, but there is a pleasant higgledy piggledy layout which lends an air or informality. The Cave is in the basement, where there are wines of good quality from top négociants, but also a number from small producers. Nothing is desperately cheap, but plenty under 35 F which is good value compared to the UK. There are numerous big-name wines from good vintages, and a number of wines that are quite difficult to get in Britain, from the Jura and Savoie amongst others. The staff are helpful and will offer you advice. The array of spirits is amazing, including old Cognacs, Armagnacs and Calvados, Whiskies, Bourbons, Eaux de Vie, Genièvre and other curiosities. On the ground floor there is an excellent selection of Belgian beers and a lot of gift boxes and presentation packs. Everything looks very attractive.

WINE BAR   LILLE   A V ECHQ

07.30-24.00, every day

LA CLOCHE
Wine only
A wine bar where you can buy bottles to take away

13 place du Théâtre
59800 Lille

Opposite the Opéra in central Lille
Tel: 20 55 35 34

City-centre parking
English spoken
Tasting in café

La Cloche is an ordinary-looking wine bar in the heart of old Lille with a good selection of wines available by the glass. Each wine may also be purchased by the bottle to take away. There is a choice of thirty different wines each month and, although the selection does not represent the best value available on the French side of the Channel, it is a pleasant, unhassled way of discovering new wines and picking up a bottle or two. There is a brasserie on the first floor where you can eat.

SMALL SHOP   LILLE   A V AMEX EC

10.30-13.00 and 14.30-19.00, Tuesday to Saturday; closed Sunday and Monday morning

NICOLAS
Wines, spirits and a few beers
Part of a good-quality chain of French wine shops

---

5 place du Lion d'Or
59800 Lille

In the centre of Lille
Tel: 20 51 17 79

City-centre limited parking
No English spoken
Selected promotional tastings

This is a small city-centre branch of the large good-quality chain of Nicolas wine shops. Nicolas has many branches all over France and even a few in London, but apart from Lille, none are in the area covered in this book. The wines are fairly up-market without a huge selection in the under-30 F range, but the quality is usually good. The best value are probably the Nicolas own-label wines. All the French regions are covered but in the city-centre shop the policy is to stock more of the lesser-known wines away from the traditional favourites of Bordeaux, hence a good selection from the Mediterranean and the south-west. There are usually promotions on, and when I visited there was a 20% discount on any quantity of all champagnes which meant good savings on most prices relative to the UK. This would be particularly worth while if buying a small quantity of something expensive like Krug, because discounts in Britain are usually for six bottles or more. Other good discounts were three for the price of two on certain bottles of good-quality wine. You really need a price list from a British store, because some but not all of these transient offers represent good savings.

LARGE SHOP   LILLE   A V AMEX EC

10.30-13.00 and 14.30-19.00, Tuesday to Saturday; closed Sunday and Monday morning

NICOLAS
Wines, spirits and a few beers
Part of a good-quality chain of French wine shops

angle Route Nationale and boulevard Georges Clemenceau
59700 Marcq-en-Baroeul

Off the N17 coming into Lille from the north
Tel: 20 55 26 13

Reasonable parking on the street
No English spoken
Selected promotional tasting

This is a much larger shop than the city-centre branch with a lot more of the wines on the Nicolas list. The location is in the suburb of Marcq-en-Baroeul which you may pass through if you are coming into Lille from the north. For a full comment see the entry above.

MEDIUM-SIZED SHOP VEURNE ECHQ

08.00-12.00 and 13.00-18.00, Monday to Friday

COULIER WIJNHANDEL
Fine wines and spirits
Few bargains for UK shoppers

Ondernemingenstraat 9
B-8630 Veurne

On the N390 just oustide Veurne
Tel: (058) 31 59 60

Private car-park
Minimal English spoken
No tasting

Coulier Wijnhandel is in an out-of-town industrial estate a few doors down the road from the Eastenders tobacco shop, but a million miles away in terms of style from the Calais bulk-buy warehouse. Here the emphasis is on quality and price is secondary. There is the usual good selection of Bordeaux and plenty from the other major French regions. The policy of the shop is to steer away from large négociants and concentrate on smaller grower/producers. Although much of what they sell is fairly expensive, at the bottom end of the range there are wines that are cheaper than you would find in the UK. Everything in the shop is well presented but the atmosphere of the place is a little bit stiff and formal. You are unlikely to want to make a special trip here, but if staying nearby it would be a place to come and pick out a classy and exclusive bottle.

VERY LARGE SUPERMARKET   NR. VEURNE ECHQ

09.00-20.00, Monday to Saturday

GB
Good range of wine, beer and spirits
Good for wines, fortified wines and Belgian beers

19 Strandlaan
8670 Koksijde

On the road from Veurne towards Koksijde beach
Tel: (058) 51 62 32

Large car-park
Some English spoken
No tasting

See entry below for GB in Bruges

SMALL SHOP   VEURNE   ECHQ

09.30-12.00 and 14.00-19.00; closed Sunday p.m. and Monday a.m.

WIJNHANDEL DE CLERCK
Fine wine and fortified wine
Small, select and expensive

Kaatsspelplaats 1
8630 Veurne

Just by the main square in central Veurne
Tel: (058) 31 51 52

Town-centre on-street parking
No English spoken
No tasting

This wine shop in the centre of Veurne has a fairly small selection of good-quality wine and fortified wine. There is very little to choose from in the under-150 FB range which is where savings on British prices are possible.

DRIVE-IN WAREHOUSE   NIEUWPOORT   ECHQ

08.30-12.00 and 13.30-18.00; closed Tuesday and Sunday

BIERHANDEL RENE DEBAL
Wine, beer and spirits
Typical Belgian drive-in

52a Albertlaan
8620 Nieuwpoort

On road out from Nieuwpoort Bad to Nieuwpoort
Tel: (058) 23 31 46

Car-park
A little English spoken
No tasting

Similar to other Belgian drive-in shops. For comment see entry for De Bierhalle Drankenservice.

DRIVE-IN WAREHOUSE   WESTENDE   ECHQ

09.00-12.30 and 14.00-19.00; closed Sunday p.m.

DE BIERHALLE DRANKENSERVICE
Wine, beer and spirits
A local drink supplier

Nieuwpoortlaan 69
8434 Westende

On the coast road between Westende and Nieuwpoort
Tel: (058) 23 41 04

Large car-park
Limited English spoken
No tasting

There are a number of these drive-in drinks stores along the coast which cater very much to local and holiday trade. There is a fairly standard range of cheaper wines and spirits and beers, but the choice is not as good as in the supermarkets and many of the beers are in returnable bottles for which a returnable deposit is paid. As with other Belgian drinks stores the prices tend to be higher than in France for most things but you can still pick up bargains relative to the UK. Certainly not worth making a detour for but possibly a last-stop place to buy beer on a Sunday morning.

LARGE SUPERMARKET   MIDDELKERKE ECHQ

10.00-19.00, Monday to Saturday; closed Sunday

COLRUYT
Wine, beer and spirits
See entry for Bruges

Oostendsesteenweg 298
8430 Middelkerke

On the coast road to Oostende
Tel: (059) 30 26 85

Large car-park
Some English spoken
A selection of wines on tasting

A good Belgian supermarket, for details see entry for Colruyt in Bruges.

LARGE SUPERMARKET   MIDDELKERKE
ECHQ

09.00-20.00, Monday to Saturday

GB
Good range of wine, beer and spirits
Good for wines, fortified wines and Belgian beers

Oostendelaan 300
8430 Middelkerke

On the main road to Oostende
Tel: (059) 30 11 94

Large car-park
Some English spoken
No tasting

A good Belgian supermarket, for comment see entry for GB in Bruges.

DRIVE-IN WAREHOUSE   MIDDELKERKE
ECHQ

09.00-12.30 and 13.30-18.00; closed Saturday from 11.00 and Sunday

DEPOT VANHOUTTE
Wine, beer and spirits
Another local drive-in

Oostendelaan 272
8430 Middelkerke

On the coast road between Middelkerke and Nieuwpoort
Tel: (059) 31 15 15

Large car-park
Limited English spoken
No tasting

Catering for local customers, this shop has a number of beers, gift packs, and a small range of wines. We did manage to find Bellevue Gueuze and Dentergems beer, however, at the reduced price of 80 FB for a pack of six which works out on the current exchange rate at about 26p a bottle. I doubt bargains like this are normally available though. Generally the choice in supermarkets is better.

LARGE SUPERMARKET   OOSTENDE   ECHQ

09.00-20.00, Monday to Saturday

DELHAIZE
Wine, beer and spirits
A good all-round supermarket selection

Leopold III Laan 7
8400 Oostende

Centre of Oostende
Tel: (059) 80 39 11

Large car-park
Some English spoken
No tasting

Belgian supermarkets stock a better selection of good quality wine than their French counterparts but their prices are correspondingly higher. While not as ecclectic as a UK supermarket, there is a very good range from outside France, mostly from Spain, Chile, Italy and Germany. The best wine bargains are under 100 FB (£2) and include wines from the south such as Côtes de Roussillon, Minervois and lesser-known ACs from the Rhône. There are plenty to choose from at under 200 FB which are nearly all cheaper than equivalents in the UK. Particular bargains were a St-Véran at 199 FB and several Bordeaux Cru Bourgeois under 250 FB. It could definitely be worth buying a bottle to taste first then getting another 24 at 10% discount. There is plenty here which is difficult to find in UK supermarkets: a good choice of reasonably priced Loire reds, wines from Luxembourg and from Savoie. As with all supermarkets look out for the promotions. If you are satisfied with a choice of a mere 30-40 Belgian beers, supermarkets like this are a good place to buy large quantities. Run of the mill beers are geared towards locals but you can pick up cases of familiar favourites, such as Stella, considerably cheaper than in the UK, but not at prices competitive with French bulk sellers. The same applies to spirits, although cheap fortified wines such as port, sherry and vermouth are cheaper than in France.

LARGE SUPERMARKET   OOSTENDE   ECHQ

09.00-20.00, Monday to Saturday

GB
Wine, beer and spirits
A large supermarket selection

Pieterslaan 85a
8400 Oostende

Centre of Oostende
Tel: (059) 80 43 37

Large car-park
Some English spoken
No tasting

See entry for GB in Bruges

SHOP   OOSTENDE   ECHQ

08.30-12.00 and 13.00-17.00; closed Saturday morning and Sunday

GENERAL STORES
Mostly wine with some fortified wine and spirits
A smart up-market wine shop

De Smet de Naeyerlaan 36
8400 Oostende

Centre of Oostende
Tel: (059) 70 25 03

Adequate on-street parking
Good English spoken
No tasting possible

This is a very smart shop with a good range of high quality wines and spirits but unfortunately few bargains for visitors from the

UK. The staff are friendly and helpful and speak good English. The attraction of a shop like this is probably just to pick up the odd bottle which would be quite difficult to find back home, such as something from the large range of Pomerol, one of the seven different Grand Cru Chablis, a white St-Amour or one of the four different Pineau de Charentes. Anything that you can find which looks familiar is likely to be cheaper in Britain.

SMALL SUPERMARKET   OOSTENDE   £ ECHQ

9.00-13.00 and 14.00-19.00; closed Sunday afternoon (and closed Monday afternoon out of season)

MAINHOUT SUPERMARKET
Beer, wine and spirits
Small centrally located supermarket with reasonable range

Groentenmarkt 1-2
8400 Oostende

Right in the centre of Oostende
Tel: (059) 80 25 60

City centre, so parking not easy
Some English spoken
No tasting

This small supermarket is unremarkable but offers a good Sunday stocking-up place in central Oostende. The range is OK and the prices are reasonable. There is a good selection of Belgian beers with Hoegaarden Grand Cru (33cl) at 33 FB, Duvel (33cl) 4-pack at 119 FB, and Corsendonk (33cl) 4-pack at 124 FB. Wines include cheap Bulgarian, Italian and German and a few reasonable looking buys from France. There is also a good selection of spirits and fortified wines which are about as cheap as you will find in this area, with Cinzano at 123 FB, Genever from 300 FB and a Calvados at 499 FB.

SMALL SHOP   OOSTENDE   EC FB

9.30-19.30; closed Wednesday and Sunday afternoon

WIJNHUIS DOUCHY
Wines and spirits
Small fine wine shop

Koningstraat 56
8400 Oostende

Central Ostend on road out to Middelkerke
Tel: (059) 70 97 23

Limited on-street parking
A little English spoken
No tasting

One of two branches (the other in Diksmuide at 1 Schoolplan) which offer a standard range of French wines and spirits. You should be able to find good examples from most regions of France. As usual Bordeaux predominates with many of the big names, although there are also a few wines under 200 FB which are cheaper than UK equivalents. They specialize in a range of their own label sparkling wines and reasonably priced white and red Bordeaux from Chateaux Séguin. Other than that there is a fair selection from the major French wine regions, although prices in Belgium are currently such that it isn't worth a special trip here just to buy wine. No beer is sold in Wijnhuis Douchy, but they have several types of the other local speciality, Genever. Along with the usual variety, there are apple- and lemon-flavoured ones with reasonable prices starting at 275 BF.

MEDIUM-SIZED SHOP   OOSTENDE   EC £ FB

9.30-12.30 and 14.00-19.00; closed Sunday afternoon

DE WIJNKELDER
Wines, beers and spirits
An interesting shop worth visiting

Groentenmarkt 3
8400 Oostende

Right in the centre of Ostend
Tel: (059) 70 81 39

Town-centre parking (reasonably difficult)
Limited English spoken
No tasting possible

This shop in the centre of Oostende has an individual selection of wines and spirits and an excellent selection of over 100 Belgian beers. The wines include not only the usual French regions but some Spanish and Italian as well. There is a good selection of bottles that are significantly cheaper than in the UK: Côtes de Gascogne for 98 FB, Alsace Pinot Gris 195 FB, and Henri de Villamont Chablis for 256 FB. You'd have difficulty in finding as good a selection of many of the fortified wines and spirits in the UK, especially the Calvados and Pineau de Charentes. There is a huge number of miniatures, including footballs, bananas, Eaux de Vie and all kinds of aperitif. The major attraction of this shop is the selection of beers, however, which is unsurpassed locally and should keep all but the most intrepid Belgian beer hunters happy. They can be bought individually, by the bottle, at very reasonable prices. There is also a fascinating range of the appropriate glasses to match the beers.

SMALL SHOP   BRUGES   ECHQ

09.30-12.30 and 13.30-16.00; closed Thursday afternoons

AD FUNDUM
Beers and old Genevers
A small specialist town-centre shop

Geldmuntstraat 46
8000 Bruges

Centre of Bruges

No nearby parking
Some English spoken
No tasting

This is a small shop with a large selection of beers including De Dolle Brouwers and some old Genevers. Worth dropping in if you are in central Bruges on the beer trail.

SMALL CAFÉ   BRUGES   BF

16.00-13.00 week (14.00 weekend)

'T BRUGS BEERTJEN BIERBOETIEK
300 Belgian beers
Speciality beer shop

Kemelstraat 5
8000 Bruges

Central Bruges

Difficult parking in central Bruges
English spoken
Beers sold in the bar

Not a shop, but a café with a great atmosphere and a fantastic selection of beers. Come here and sample, to work out what you have a taste for in the Belgian beer department.

SMALL CAFÉ   BRUGES   BF

16.00-13.00 week (14.00 weekend); closed Monday and Tuesday

BISTRO DREUPEL HUISJE '1919'
100 sorts of Genevers and liqueurs
Speciality shop and cafâ

Kemelstraat 9
8000 Bruges

Central Bruges

Difficult parking in central Bruges
English spoken
Genever and beer sold in the bar

Next door to the café above is this one which specializes in beer
and Genever. Another place it is difficult to leave completely
sober.

LARGE SUPERMARKET BRUGES ECHQ

10.00-19.00, Monday to Saturday; closed Sunday

COLRUYT
Wine, beer and spirits
A good all-round supermarket

Gistelsesteenweg 345
8200 St-Andries
Bruges

Off road out of Bruges in direction of Lille
Tel: (050) 38 95 58

Large car-park
English spoken
A selection of wines on tasting

Don't be deceived by the gloomy Kwik Save no-frills look to these supermarkets because Colruyt has a good-quality selection of wines. They have quite a large list of mainly French wines priced from 85 FB to 1,000 FB. At Colruyt you can ring a bell to call to get advice about the wine and there is usually someone there who can speak English. The prices are a little bit confusing because with most beers and many wines you are charged for the bottles and get the deposit back on return. The pricing seems to be on a par with other Belgian supermarkets; the wines and spirits are more expensive than in France but the Belgian beers and fortified wines are cheaper. The tasting facility and the availability of advice make this an attractive place to shop although the range of drink is a bit smaller than in the GB or Delhaize.

LARGE SUPERMARKET   BRUGES   ECHQ

09.00-20.00, Monday to Saturday

DELHAIZE
Wine, beer and spirits
A good all-round supermarket selection

Malesteenweg 234
8310 St-Kruis
Bruges

Off N9 road out of Bruges in direction of Gent
Tel: (050) 35 59 48

Large car-park
Some English spoken
No tasting

See entry for Delhaize in Oostende section

BREWERY BRUGES ECHO

07.00-12.00 and 12.30-17.00, Monday to Friday

DE GOUDEN BOOM
Beer only
A place to buy beer brewed on site

Langestraat 45
8000 Bruges

Central Bruges
Tel: (050) 33 06 99

English spoken
Tasting included with tour
Beer only

This is more of a working brewery than Straffe Hendrik listed below. Visits are arranged by prior appointment for 15-100 people with an English-speaking guide, and cost 150 FB including a sample of the beer. If there are too few of you to join a group let them know when you are coming, because there is a good chance you will be able to join in with another party. You can also buy the beer by the crate cheaper here than anywhere else. Four beers are available: Brugs Tarwebier (wheat beer), Brugse Triple and Steenbrugge Double and Triple. These are wonderful traditionally made beers going for rock-bottom prices. They also sell the glasses which match each of the beers, magnums and gift packs. Try the beers locally, and if you like them this is the place to buy in quantity.

SMALL SHOP   BRUGES   ECHQ

8.00-12.00 and 1.30-18.30; closed Sunday

HUIS COSAERT DELHAIZE
Few wines, beers and spirits
Touristy shop in central Bruges

Markt 35
8000 Bruges

Central square in Bruges
Tel: (050) 33 39 35

Difficult parking in central Bruges
Good English spoken
No tasting

A funny general store right on the Groentemarkt, where it is strange to see whisky next to toilet paper, and wine next to toothpaste. There is a small selection of quite expensive wines, and a good range of spirits, including miniatures and local specialities. This shop has a lot of Belgian beers, with many gift packs and magnums. The Belgian beers are quite reasonably priced considering the location of the shop which is in the heart of old Bruges. Another similar shop called Missault is to be found at 5 Braambergstraat, also in the centre of Bruges, where the opening hours are 08.30-19.00 every day. Here you will find your wine, beer and spirits mixed up with cigars, pralines and other household goods.

SUPERMARKET   BRUGES   ECHQ

9.00-18.30, Monday to Saturday

NOPRI
Wines, beers and spirits
Medium-sized supermarket with fairly standard range

Noordzandstraat 4
8000 Bruges

Central Bruges
Tel: (050) 34 16 12

Difficult parking in central Bruges
No English spoken
No tasting

These supermarkets offer a number of wines for under 200 FB which are cheaper than in the UK and Belgian beers cheaper than in the souvenir and tourist shops. Similar to the above are two branches of the EDI supermarket chain at 55 Langestraat (open 09.00-12.30 and 13.30-18.30; closed on Sunday) and a smaller version at 17 Langerei (open 09.00-12.30 and 14.00-18.00; closed on Sunday).

SMALL BREWERY   BRUGES   ECHQ

10.00-17.00, every day

STRAFFE HENDRIK
Beer only
An opportunity to visit a brewery

Walplein 26
8000 Bruges

Centre of Bruges
Tel: (050) 33 26 97

No nearby parking
English spoken
Tasting included with tour

Visits are arranged with an English-speaking guide between 10.00 and 17.00 (April-September) and between 11.00 and 15.00 during the rest of the year. The brewery is now more of a museum, with just one beer still made here. There is an opportunity to sample the beer and see a great view of the town included in the 120 FB admission price. You can continue sampling the beer at your leisure and your own expense in the bar afterwards. If you like the Straffe Hendrik beer, you can buy it for 650 BF for a case of 24 x 25cl bottles or 850 BF for a case of 12 x 75cl bottles. This is probably cheaper than anywhere else.

LARGE SUPERMARKET   BRUGES   ECHQ

09.00-20.00, Monday to Saturday

GB
Good range of wine, beer and spirits
Good for wines, fortified wines and Belgian beers

Gistelsteenweg 344
8200 St-Andries
Bruges

Off road out of Bruges in direction of Lille
Tel: (050) 40 46 11

Large car-park
Some English spoken
No tasting

When I asked a bar owner where the best place to buy Belgian beer in Bruges was, she said GB. Along with Belgian beer there was a large range of most of the alcoholic drinks that one would normally want to buy. There are plenty of promotions which are worth looking out for and a large choice of wines in most categories, well laid out and easy to find. GB has more non-French wine than most other places I saw, and a good selection of bottles familiar to UK shoppers from Spain, Italy, California and Bulgaria. There were also some nice, unusual choices such as sweet Hungarian Tokay Aszu, and plenty to choose from for under 200 FB: St-Chinian, Corbières and Gigondas. GB has tons of different rosés, plenty of lesser Bordeaux and there was a selection of reasonably priced Alsace from the reliable Pfaffenheim Co-op. You get the impression that Belgian supermarkets choose their wine with a lot more care than the French and the extra you spend here is likey to be rewarded with better quality.

LARGE SUPERMARKET   BRUGES   ECHQ

09.00-20.00, Monday to Saturday

GB
Good range of wine, beer and spirits
Good for wines, fortified wines and Belgian beers

Scheepsdaelelaan 3
8000 Bruges

Off the N9 road out of Bruges in direction of Oostende
Tel: (050) 31 50 95

Large car-park
Some English spoken
No tasting

See GB entry above

VERY LARGE SUPERMARKET   BRUGES   ECHQ

09.00-20.00, Monday to Saturday

GB
Good range of wine, beer and spirits
Good for wines, fortified wines and Belgian beers

Malesteenweg 334
8310 St-Kruis
Bruges

Off N9 road out of Bruges in direction of Gent
Tel: (050) 35 18 41

Large car-park
Some English spoken
No tasting

This is a larger version of the GB described above.

Going through the Tunnel

There are two services which use the Channel Tunnel: Eurostar, the high-speed passenger train link between London and Paris or Brussels, and Le Shuttle which is a 'turn up and go service' for cars and other vehicles.

Eurostar is run by the European Passenger Service which is owned jointly by BR and the French railways, SNCF and SNCB. Information about the service is available from BR, the SNCF (in France), or the Eurostar Information Line (0233 617 525).

Le Shuttle has been designed for the maximum convenience of people travelling by car. The terminals on both sides of the Channel are very clearly signposted from the motorway. In England, you turn off the M20 at junction 11A just before you get to Folkestone. On the French side the terminal is situated at junction 13 on the A26 just outside Calais in the direction of Boulogne.

Tickets can be bought directly from toll booths at each terminal where English and French cash, cheques, and major direct debit and credit cards are all accepted. You can buy your ticket in advance from Le Shuttle Customer Service Centre and many ABTA travel agents, but prior reservation of departure time is not possible.

Once you have your ticket, you can either head for Le Shuttle or stop off in the terminal building and do some duty free shopping or have a meal. There is a good selection of shops and restaurants and a bureau de change. On your way to Le Shuttle you pass through both French and British frontier controls. This is a major innovation - the only place in the world where you have one nation's frontier controls on the soil of another. It is a great help, speeding things up considerably on the other side of the Channel.

Having cleared the frontier controls, you drive to the allocation area where you wait to be directed onto Le Shuttle. You then drive down a ramp and are directed on board. If you are travelling in a car of under 1.85 metres high, you will travel in a double-deck carriage and may be directed on to the top or bottom deck. Once on board you drive through the carriages until an attendant tells you where to stop. You are instructed to put on the handbrake, leave the car in gear and open a window. All the staff working on Le Shuttle speak both French and English.

The journey itself takes about half an hour. You can get out of your car and wander about in the carriage or stay inside and listen to Le Shuttle radio service. Once through the Tunnel, having already passed frontier controls, you drive straight off and are on the motorway or autoroute almost immediately. The whole journey is incredibly smooth and easy.

There will be a minimum of one shuttle per hour throughout the night, but this will rise to four per hour at peak times. For Le Shuttle information and ticket sales, phone 01303 271100 in the UK, or 21 00 61 00 in France.

APPENDIX 2

Recommendations

Drinks

5 light-bodied red wines and rosé:
* Bordeaux Clairet (rosé), page 25
* Gaillac (red), page 79
* VDP Jardin de la France (red and rosé), page 53
* Côtes de Duras (red), page 78
* St. Chinian (red), page 88

5 medium-bodied red wines:
* Chinon, page 52
* Côtes de Castillon, page 27
* Canon-Fronsac, page 26
* Hautes-Côtes de Nuits, page 43
* Premières Côtes de Blaye, page 33

5 full-bodied red wines:
* Minervois, page 87
* St-Joseph, page 68
* Gigondas, page 66
* Corbières, page 84
* Cahors, page 77

5 dry white wines:
* VDP Côtes de Gascogne, page 79
* Ménétou-Salon, page 54
* St-Véran, page 45
* Pinot Blanc d'Alsace, page 73
* Bergerac, page 77

5 sweet white wines:
* Côteaux du Layon, page 52
* Monbazillac, page 81
* Ste Croix-du-Mont, page 34

* Cadillac, page 25
* Vouvray, page 59

5 sparkling wines:
* New World Sparkling, page 120
* Saumur, page 118
* Blanquette de Limoux, page 115
* Crémant de Bourgogne, page 117
* Clairette de Die, page 116

5 fortified wines:
* Muscat de Rivesaltes, page 131
* Banyuls, page 131
* Chambery, page 131
* Ratafia, page 131
* Pineau de Charente, page 134

5 spirits:
* Calvados du Pays d'Auge, page 133
* Eau de Vie de Fleur de Bière, page 133
* Genièvre de Houlle, page 133
* Armagnac, page 132
* Eau de Vie de Cidre, page 133

5 beers:
* 3 Monts, page 128
* Hoegaarden Grand Cru, page 127
* Orval, page 127
* Jenlain, page 128
* Morte Subite Gueuze, page 127

OUTLETS

5 specialist shops:
* **Cave Paul Herpe** specializes in wines from Languedoc-Roussillon, branches in Dunkerque, Boulogne and Berck, pages: 207, 178, 187
* **Royal Champagne** specializes in champagne. Shop in Calais, page 155
* **Noel Cuvelier's Beer Shop** specializes in beer. Shop in

Poperinge, Belgium, page 214

* **Caves du Producteur** specializes in red Bordeaux. Shops in Bruay, page 169; St-Omer, page 164; and Lievin, page 170
* **Le Terroir specializes** in unusual spirits. Shop in Wimereux, page 174

5 general wine shops:
* **Chais de la Transat** in Dunkerque, page 209
* **Grape Shop** in Boulogne, pages 179, 180
* **Caves St. Arnould** in St-Omer, page 164
* **Les Caves du Vieux Chais** in Fressin, page 193
* **Peradel** in Calais, page 153

5 bulk sales shops:
* **Le Chais** in Calais, page 146 and Boulogne, page 181
* **Calais Wine and Beer** in Calais, page 143
* **Cash and Carry B & B** in Calais, page 144
* **Beers R Us** in Calais, page 142
* **Eastenders** in Calais, page 149

5 hypermarkets;
* **Hyper Cedico**, St-Omer, page 162
* **Mammouth**, Calais, page 152
* **Hyper Auchan**, Boulogne, page 168
* **Carrefour**, Dunkerque, page 205
* **Continent**, Calais, page 148

APPENDIX 3

Main French Grape Types

RED GRAPES

* **Cabernet Sauvignon** is the world's favourite red grape. It has good colour, gives a blackcurrant aroma and flavour, and is fairly high in acid and tannins. It is used extensively in Bordeaux where it produces medium- to full-bodied wines which age very well. Cabernet Franc is similar, but a little lighter in body and colour, and produces a more grassy, lighter fruit flavour.

* **Gamay** produces light-bodied, easy-drinking wines with light fruity flavours. They are immediately appealing wines that are made to be drunk young. Beaujolais is the best-known example.

* **Merlot** is the other main Bordeaux grape, which produces richer, softer, more plummy flavours. The wines are slightly more alcoholic and are less suited to long periods of ageing than those from Cabernet Sauvignon.

* **Pinot Noir** is the main grape of Burgundy, where it produces lighter-coloured wines than Cabernet Sauvignon. They have a strawberry and raspberry fruitiness when young, and are deceptively full bodied. They age well to produce wines with a complex vegetal character.

* **Syrah** produces full-bodied, dark wines with spicy, rich berried fruit character. The wines are capable of ageing very well, are used in the best Rhônes and some of the better wines from the south.

* **Southern Grapes** include Cinsault, Mourvedre, Carignan and Grenache. They are used in a blend in the southern Rhône and many of the areas further south. The wines vary in character, but are generally medium to full bodied, and produce warm fruit

flavours. Depending on the mix of grapes, they may be capable of ageing. These grapes are often mixed with Syrah to add extra richness to the wines.

WHITE GRAPES

* **Chardonnay** was originally the Burgundy grape, but is now grown almost everywhere. The wines have good body, a buttery texture and good acidity and fruit character. They are often oak-aged, which makes them less fresh but enhances the richness and butteriness of their character, and adds a variety of complex flavours.

* **Chenin Blanc** is a major Loire grape, producing very acidic wines with a flowery, honeyed character. They are made dry or sweet, and become interesting and complex when aged in oak.

* **Sauvignon Blanc**, also from the Loire, produces very acidic dry wines with green, gooseberry flavours. They are refreshing and delicious, and best drunk young.

* **Sémillon** produces flowery charactered, full-bodied wines. The grapes complement Sauvignon Blanc well and are often used together in blends. Sémillon grapes are also capable of producing fantastic sweet wines, the most famous example being Sauternes.

Other grapes are described in the relevant sections on wines.

APPENDIX 4

Glossary of Wine Terms

* **Acid** - A desirable component in wine if correctly balanced. It gives a wine its refreshing quality

* **Big** - Can mean intensely flavoured or full bodied or both

* **Blanc de Blancs** - White wine made from white grapes

* **Body** - The feel or weight a wine has in the mouth

* **Botrytis** - Otherwise known as 'noble rot', this is a rot which is desirable on grapes intended for the production of sweet wines. It extracts water, making the grapes sweeter and more concentrated

* **Brut** - Name used to describe dry sparkling wines. Extra Brut means bone-dry

* **Claret** - Red wine from Bordeaux

* **Complex** - This is a desirable attribute of wine which has taken on a variety of flavours and characteristics

* **Crémant** - A softer, sparkling wine

* **Demi-Sec** - Although the name suggests fairly dry wines, Demi-Sec actually describes sweet sparkling wines

* **Doux** - A word used in many different types of drink, meaning sweet

* **Elevé en Fûts de Chene** - Aged in oak barrels

* **Moelleux** - Extremely sweet

* **Mousseux** - Sparkling

* **Négociant** - Wine merchant

* **Structure** - The frame or skeleton of the wine that the flavour hangs on to

* **Sur Lie** - This means 'on the lees', which means that the maturing wine has been left in contact with its sediment for a prolonged period before bottling. This can enhance the body and flavour of an otherwise neutral wine

* **Tannin** - A component of red wine which gives structure and allows ageing. If there is too much tannin, a wine becomes harsh and astringent

* **Varietal** - The type of grape. Varietal labelling is where the main name on the label is a grape type, rather than a region or a particular producer. Varietal labelling is common for Vin de Pays, and wines from the New World and Eastern Europe

* **Vintage** - The year in which the grapes were harvested. Vintage wines are wines produced with the grapes from a single year. Non-vintage wines are made with a blend of grapes from various years